T0395223

OPTIONS TRADING

FROM **UNDERSTANDING THE TYPES OF OPTIONS** AND **CREATING A TRADE PLAN** TO **ANALYZING RISK** AND **SELECTING STRIKE PRICES, AN** ESSENTIAL PRIMER IN OPTIONS TRADING

101

JAMES ROYAL, PhD

ADAMS MEDIA

New York Amsterdam/Antwerp London Toronto Sydney/Melbourne New Delhi

Adams Media
An Imprint of Simon & Schuster, LLC
100 Technology Center Drive
Stoughton, MA 02072

For more than 100 years, Simon & Schuster has championed authors and the stories they create. By respecting the copyright of an author's intellectual property, you enable Simon & Schuster and the author to continue publishing exceptional books for years to come. We thank you for supporting the author's copyright by purchasing an authorized edition of this book.

No amount of this book may be reproduced or stored in any format, nor may it be uploaded to any website, database, language-learning model, or other repository, retrieval, or artificial intelligence system without express permission. All rights reserved. Inquiries may be directed to Simon & Schuster, 1230 Avenue of the Americas, New York, NY 10020 or permissions@simonandschuster.com.

Copyright © 2025 by
Simon & Schuster, LLC.

All rights reserved, including the right to reproduce this book or portions thereof in any form whatsoever. For information, address Adams Media Subsidiary Rights Department, 1230 Avenue of the Americas, New York, NY 10020.

First Adams Media hardcover edition
July 2025

ADAMS MEDIA and colophon are registered trademarks of Simon & Schuster, LLC.

Simon & Schuster strongly believes in freedom of expression and stands against censorship in all its forms. For more information, visit BooksBelong.com.

For information about special discounts for bulk purchases, please contact Simon & Schuster Special Sales at 1-866-506-1949 or business@simonandschuster.com.

The Simon & Schuster Speakers Bureau can bring authors to your live event. For more information or to book an event, contact the Simon & Schuster Speakers Bureau at 1-866-248-3049 or visit our website at www.simonspeakers.com.

Manufactured in the United States of America

1 2025

Library of Congress Control Number: 2025935412

ISBN 978-1-5072-2403-8
ISBN 978-1-5072-2404-5 (ebook)

Many of the designations used by manufacturers and sellers to distinguish their products are claimed as trademarks. Where those designations appear in this book and Simon & Schuster, LLC, was aware of a trademark claim, the designations have been printed with initial capital letters.

This publication is designed to provide accurate and authoritative information with regard to the subject matter covered. It is sold with the understanding that the publisher is not engaged in rendering legal, accounting, or other professional advice. If legal advice or other expert assistance is required, the services of a competent professional person should be sought.
—From a *Declaration of Principles* jointly adopted by a Committee of the American Bar Association and a Committee of Publishers and Associations

CONTENTS

INTRODUCTION 6

CHAPTER 1: OPTIONS OVERVIEW **8**

WHAT IS OPTIONS TRADING?. 9

HOW OPTIONS WORK. 13

ADVANTAGES AND DISADVANTAGES OF OPTIONS. 17

ARE OPTIONS TOO RISKY? YES AND NO 22

IS OPTIONS TRADING FOR YOU? 26

A FOUNDATIONAL UNDERSTANDING OF INVESTING 30

WHAT YOU'LL NEED TO TRADE OPTIONS. 35

CHAPTER 2: THE FUNDAMENTALS OF OPTIONS **39**

KEY NEED-TO-KNOW OPTIONS TERMS 40

CALL OPTIONS: REWARDS AND RISKS 44

PUT OPTIONS: REWARDS AND RISKS 49

INTRINSIC VALUE VERSUS TIME VALUE 54

WHAT AN OPTION IS WORTH 58

KEY DRIVERS OF OPTIONS PRICES: THE GREEKS. 62

HOW OPTION PRICES MOVE 67

PUT-CALL PARITY. 72

KEY OPTIONS STYLES 77

HOW ARE OPTIONS TAXED?. 82

CHAPTER 3: HOW TO TRADE OPTIONS 87

DEVELOPING AN INVESTMENT THESIS 88

FINDING THE RIGHT OPTIONS STRATEGY 93

LEARN TO READ THE OPTIONS CHAIN 97

PLACING YOUR OPTIONS TRADE 102

LEGGING INTO OPTIONS TRADES. 106

WHEN AND HOW TO EXIT YOUR OPTIONS TRADE 110

BUILDING AN INVESTMENT PORTFOLIO WITH OPTIONS. 114

HOW OPTIONS TRADERS FAIL 119

CHAPTER 4: BASIC OPTIONS STRATEGIES 124

LONG CALL 125

SHORT CALL 131

LONG PUT. 137

SHORT PUT 143

DON'T OVERLOOK BASIC OPTIONS STRATEGIES 149

CHAPTER 5: INTERMEDIATE AND ADVANCED
OPTIONS STRATEGIES 153

COVERED CALL 154

PROTECTIVE PUT 159

SYNTHETIC LONG 164

SYNTHETIC SHORT. 169

LONG STRADDLE 174

SHORT STRADDLE 179

LONG STRANGLE 184

SHORT STRANGLE 189

COLLAR 194

CHAPTER 6: SPREAD OPTIONS STRATEGIES **199**

PROS AND CONS OF SPREAD OPTIONS STRATEGIES 200
VERTICAL, HORIZONTAL, AND DIAGONAL SPREADS 204
BULL CALL SPREAD 209
BEAR PUT SPREAD 214
BEAR CALL SPREAD 219
BULL PUT SPREAD 224
LONG CALENDAR SPREAD WITH CALLS 229
LONG DIAGONAL SPREAD WITH CALLS 234

CHAPTER 7: MORE MULTI-LEG SPREAD OPTIONS
  STRATEGIES **239**

LONG BUTTERFLY SPREAD WITH CALLS 240
SHORT BUTTERFLY SPREAD WITH CALLS 245
LONG IRON BUTTERFLY SPREAD 249
LONG CONDOR SPREAD WITH CALLS 254
SHORT CONDOR SPREAD WITH CALLS 259

CHAPTER 8: TROUBLESHOOTING OPTIONS TRADING **264**

HOW TO PIVOT WHEN THE MARKET SHIFTS 265
HOW TO HANDLE SETBACKS 269
KEEPING EMOTIONS OUT OF TRADING 273
SETTING REALISTIC GOALS 278

INDEX 283

INTRODUCTION

If you've ever been curious about the interesting world of options trading, look no further. Options are one of the fastest-growing areas of the financial markets and for good reason: They offer you the potential to make money quickly. However, options can move more quickly than other investment types and can be highly volatile, so those looking to trade need a strong foundation before they begin.

Options Trading 101 teaches how options work and how to make money trading them. This book also covers how and when to close your options position, how to manage options risks, and how to handle common setbacks eventually faced by all traders. In short, this book walks you through the basics and beyond, with topics ranging from:

- The fundamentals of options, including how options are structured and their key risks and rewards
- The four core options strategies, including examples and how to fine-tune your risk and return
- Advanced options strategies that you can use to generate profits with reduced risk
- How options are priced, what drives their price, and how to anticipate their price changes
- Common pitfalls of options trading and how to avoid them
- The important options trading vocabulary, so that you can speak confidently and knowledgeably
- And more!

Whether you're a novice options trader looking to learn the ropes, or a more experienced trader looking to review the basics, this book has something for you. Of course, if you do happen to be a novice trader, you should have a solid background in investing and understand how stocks and securities work. That said, whatever your experience with options trading is, this book approaches options using an easy-to-understand style that explains the core concepts in detail. It then uses examples to show you how fascinating options are, how they work in practice, and how you can calibrate your options trading to your desired risk level. You'll walk away from this book with a variety of strategies that you can use to make money in any market—and you'll know their potential rewards and risks.

Whichever options you focus on, you'll soon understand why this form of trading is so fascinating and use *Options Trading 101* to help guide you along your trading journey. So, turn the page and begin.

Chapter 1

Options Overview

Options open a whole new world for people like you who are looking to juice their profits from the financial markets. While options may be based on assets that you're already familiar with—stocks, exchange-traded funds (ETFs), and stock indexes—options present an entirely new set of securities and strategies, an entirely new set of risks and rewards, and an entirely new vocabulary to master. But for those who master options, the upside can be immense; as a knowledgeable trader, you can multiply your money quickly—at the risk of losing it all if you're wrong.

To capture the potential profit, you need to understand how options work, the advantages and disadvantages of options, and what you'll need to begin trading. Of course, you need to understand the many risks of options, but you'll also need to know how options can reduce your risk—an often-overlooked benefit. Ultimately, you'll need to understand all these features before deciding whether options are right for you.

WHAT IS OPTIONS TRADING?

Understanding the Principles

Options are one of the most exciting areas of the financial markets but paradoxically also one of the least understood. Options have the potential to deliver serious wealth to people who can master them, and that's why options trading is so popular among sophisticated investors. As an options trader, you can make—and lose—a fortune in just weeks or months due to the highly volatile nature of options. Plus, there are a variety of strategies to thrive in the options market while minimizing your risk, and as a savvy operator, you can learn how to navigate the options markets to take advantage of this.

OPTIONS ARE DERIVATIVES

Options are one kind of financial derivative, which is a way of saying that their price "derives" from or is based on the price of another asset. Options are often based on stocks, exchange-traded funds, and indexes, and when the prices of those underlying assets change, so do the prices of the options on them. When trading, you'll try to anticipate these moves in the market so that you're buying options that are poised to rise or selling the ones that are ready to fall in value. To do so, you'll trade options based on your expectations of how the underlying assets will perform. If you're right, the option may increase in value much faster than the stock or fund it's based on, and the speed of earning a profit is part of the huge appeal of options trading.

OPTIONS REQUIRE CONTRACTS

Options are structured as a standardized contract, with contractual terms that are similar from option to option. Each contract represents 100 shares of the stock or fund it's based on. Options exist for a finite period, which is specified in the contract when you trade it. Then when an option reaches its expiration, it ceases to exist, and the terms of the contract are settled between the option's buyer and seller. So, when you purchase or sell an option, you know exactly what you're getting. Standardized options trades are conducted on public exchanges, helping to offer transparent pricing for traders.

OPTIONS HAVE TIME LIMITS

With options trading, you're buying and selling risk over a predetermined period that you and another trader both agree on. In a real sense, you're simply buying and selling parts of an asset's returns above or below a certain stock price over a limited period. One trader might want a certain type of risk—say, a stock's returns above $40 per share for the next six months—and another is willing to sell that risk for a price.

OPTIONS ARE RISKY

You might hear the word *risk* and think of only negative things, but with options and other financial securities you should think about risk as both a positive and a negative. Sure, there are risks with negative consequences. However, without risk you have no potential for return either. The financial markets constantly price risk and return, with traders generally offering low returns for low risks and higher returns for higher risks. It follows that you must take some risk to make a return. So, you'll ultimately want to take good risks that can deliver attractive returns and be on the hunt for mispriced risk. Because of the limited duration of options contracts, you own that risk only for the length of the contract and then must repurchase the risk if you want that exposure again.

OPTIONS PROVIDE MULTIPLE PATHS TO PROFITS

Options trading can allow you to make money in virtually any kind of environment, whether the stock is moving up, down, or even sideways. The beauty of options is that they allow you to buy and sell various parts of a stock's return profile, at least over a period. Different types of options can be stacked together to get exactly the kind of risk profile that you want. If you expect a certain risk is unlikely to come to pass you can simply sell that risk to another trader who thinks it could happen. This quality makes options so wonderfully flexible and so potentially lucrative but also often misunderstood.

OPTIONS TRADES ALWAYS HAVE A WINNER AND LOSER

While options may be based on stocks, the two types of financial securities differ in fundamental ways. A stock is an ownership stake in a company, which is issued by the company to fund its operations.

A stock can exist indefinitely, if the company remains financially viable. But when an option contract expires, the bet is settled, and only one side can come out a winner, making options trading a zero-sum game. Either an option's buyer or seller comes out the winner on every transaction. Of course, brokerages that charge a commission for options trading do profit on every trade.

Lucrative Side Bets

Investing in stocks need not be a zero-sum game as the company grows and increases profits for all its shareholders. In contrast, an option is effectively a "side bet" between traders on how a stock or fund will perform over the duration of the option contract.

OPTIONS REQUIRE ACTIVE MANAGEMENT

Stocks and options differ in how you manage them. Because stocks can exist indefinitely, as an investor, you can purchase a stock and hold it for literally decades as long as it continues to exist. You can take a buy-and-hold approach to this potentially long-lived asset and may look at its performance only once or twice a year, though stocks are frequently traded with a much shorter holding period, of course. In contrast, options positions must be actively managed, with you evaluating a contract's risk and return, determining when to sell at an optimum time, and generally keeping a close eye on what's moving the positions. While you can be successful with stocks by taking a passive approach, options trading needs active management, requiring more time and attention to be successful.

HOW OPTIONS WORK

Understanding the Operation of Options

Options allow you to buy or sell an asset at a predetermined price for a period. One type of option, a call option, governs the buying—and one option, a put option, governs the selling. While these types of options contracts entitle their owners to do different things, in other fundamental respects they operate similarly.

CALL OPTIONS AND PUT OPTIONS

The buyer of a call option is entitled to purchase the underlying asset, often a stock, at a preset price for the duration of the contract. The seller of a call option is obligated to sell that asset at the agreed-upon price, regardless of how unfavorable the price is, if the buyer exercises the option. For this advantage, the call buyer pays a fee to the seller.

The buyer of a put option is entitled to sell the underlying asset, often a stock, at a preset price for the length of the contract. The seller of a put option is obligated to buy that asset at the agreed-upon price, regardless of how unfavorable the price is, if the put buyer exercises the option. For this advantage, the put buyer pays a fee to the seller.

Each contract allows an option owner to transact 100 shares of the underlying stock up until the time the option expires. If you purchase one call, you're entitled to buy 100 shares of the stock at the preset price, while six options get you exposure to 600 shares and so on. Options prices are always quoted in per-share amounts ($1.50, $2.25, $3.00, and so on) rather than the total cost of the contract, which is the per-share value times 100 shares (or $150, $225, $300, and so on).

Expectations of Buying and Selling Options

If you own an unexpired option, you have the right, but not the obligation, to exercise it and derive any advantages from it. However, if you sold the option to open a position, you're obligated to perform the actions specified in the contract, namely to buy or sell an asset at the preset price.

Options are known as "wasting assets," a term that means their value tends to decline over time. A contract with more time until expiration has more value than the same contract with less time to expiration, reflecting the former's potential to move more. A portion of the value of every option reflects how much time is left on the contract, up until the option expires. Of course, a rise in the underlying stock or a change in other variables can make the option price move up at any time, but the option's total potential is waning day by day.

HOW OPTIONS ARE SETTLED

After an options position is started, how is it finally settled? A trade is concluded in one of three ways:

A trader closes the position. As long as the option has not expired, the buyer or seller of the option can close the position at any time and remove all contractual rights and obligations. For example, if you bought an option to start a position, you would simply sell the option for the going market value, closing the position and ending any rights conferred by the option. Similarly, if you sold an option to start a position, you would repurchase the option from any willing trader, closing the position and ending any obligations. A buyer and seller need not close the position with the person they originally opened the position with, and they can purchase or sell the same option from any trader willing to make a deal. But they'll have to pay whatever the fair market value is at the time, which may be more or less than they originally transacted at.

The option is exercised. An option's owner can exercise that option at any point if the option has not expired. If a call option is exercised, the call's owner purchases the stock from the seller at the contractual price. If the seller does not own the stock, the brokerage will purchase the stock at the market rate and deliver it to the option buyer. If a put option is exercised, the put's owner sells the stock at the preset price to the put's seller. Traders are not likely to exercise an option unless it's worth some money and less than a week or two remain until the option expires, at which point it has little potential or "time value" left. If the option expires and is worth more than $0.05, the brokerage usually automatically exercises it.

The option expires worthless. If the option expires worthless, the option seller keeps the whole fee for selling the option, and the buyer ends up with nothing. The brokerage removes the worthless security from the traders' accounts by the next trading day.

OPTIONS AND LEVERAGE

Options are appealing to traders because they offer what is known as *leverage*. This term means that an option's price can move a lot in response to a stock's price movement. Because of leverage, you can put up a little bit of money in an option and have a large gain, even if the stock moves only a few percent. Here's an example to see how it works.

Imagine a stock trading for $60. A call option is available enabling the purchase of the stock for $62.50, and the option costs $1.50. So, for a cost of $1.50, the option buyer has the right to purchase the stock for $62.50. If the stock rises to $65.50 at the option's expiration, the option would be worth $3. The option's owner can purchase the stock for $62.50 from the option's seller and sell it for $65.50, for a $3 gain per share. In effect, the buyer purchases the option for $150 ($1.50 × 100) and its value doubles to $300, though the stock itself increased only about 9%, from $60 to $65.50.

OPTION SELLER RESULTS

The option seller must deliver the stock to the buyer, and the brokerage makes the delivery automatically. If the seller does not own the stock, the brokerage purchases it on the seller's behalf, charges the seller the market value of $65.50, and settles the option. In effect, the option seller buys the stock for $65.50, then sells it to the option buyer for $62.50, taking a loss of $3 on this part of the transaction. The seller initially received $1.50 for selling the option, so the seller lost $1.50 per share (or $150 overall) on this trade, the $3 loss offset by the $1.50 received from the option buyer.

ADVANTAGES AND DISADVANTAGES OF OPTIONS
The Good and Bad of Trading

Options provide a lot of, well . . . options for investors, making this trading especially attractive for intermediate and advanced investors who know their way around the market. Their flexibility means that options provide various ways to make money, generating capital gains or regular income. Options also allow you to limit risk and hedge a portfolio, and they let you make money in any market—up, down, or sideways. These advantages, of course, are balanced against some important disadvantages, in particular the potential for significant and even catastrophic loss if you don't know what you're doing.

ADVANTAGES OF OPTIONS

The following are seven major benefits of options trading, as this form of trading offers many ways to make money.

Ability to Multiply Your Money

The most attractive feature of options is the ability to rapidly multiply your money. Yes, with the right options strategy you can double or triple your money and more, sometimes in months and on rare occasions even weeks or days. Though it's not easy and you run the risk of total loss, it can be done with some knowledge and a little luck.

Ability to Trade Risk

Options allow you to buy and sell the risk of stock price movement for certain periods of time. You can carve off just the piece of risk that they're willing to buy or sell, and you decide the period you're willing to own it. You can choose to purchase the riskiest parts of a stock's potential return profile and perhaps generate significant gains, or you can stick to relatively safe areas and generate more likely but lower profits.

Tremendous Flexibility

Options can provide tremendous flexibility. Because they mimic the moves of stock positions, these financial derivatives can be sliced and diced to create the risk exposure (and payoff) that you want. You can set up any number of options strategies that can be "overlaid" on how you expect the stock to perform. You can use options to generate income or capital gains and limit risks while this trading achieves stock-like returns or better.

Generate Incremental Income from Your Stock Positions

Options can also be useful to generate income in other ways. For example, you can sell options on stocks you already own to create income. With the option, you promise to sell the stock at a specific price by a specific time. If the stock does not reach that price in the time, you keep the stock and can repeat the trade again and again.

Hedge Risks in Your Portfolio

Not only do options help you shoot for the moon, but they can also be used to hedge risks in your portfolio, reducing the impact of individual stocks. You can purchase options that completely offset the bad performance of a given stock, at least for some time.

Set Up Regular Income by Acting As an Insurer

Options can also be used to act like insurance. By selling certain types of options, you promise to purchase stock at a specific price for a specific period. By acting as insurance for stock prices, these options trades can generate regular income. Keep in mind that if the insurance is not needed, the option expires worthless, and you pocket the whole "insurance" premium. Repeat this strategy over and over, and you can generate regular income, often at low risk.

Limit Risk on Trades

Options can also be used to limit risk on trades. For example, a risky stock may offer a wide variety of returns, but to profit you would have to put up substantial cash. However, options allow you to participate in the upside by investing a much lower amount of money. So, you can limit your overall risk to a defined amount on a specific trade while still participating in potential gains.

DISADVANTAGES OF OPTIONS

At this point, options trading may seem like a great idea, but it comes with potential risks of which you should be aware. Here are five ways options trading may not be as advantageous as initially thought.

Your Thesis and Timing Must Be Right

When trading options you must be right twice. Your investment thesis must be correct, and it must be realized before your option expires. If not, you could end up losing a lot of money. Even if your thesis turns out to be correct in the fullness of time, it's worthless to your options position. Options make the already difficult job of predicting stock movements into a nightmare by adding on a time constraint.

High Cost

Options are relatively high cost, because they build into their price a variety of potential outcomes. For example, it might not be unusual for a relatively risky option that exists for only six or eight months to cost 10% of the stock's price and yet have the potential to be worthless at the end of that time. The flip side is that traders take advantage of this situation by selling options when they are relatively high cost.

Time Slowly Eats Away the Option's Value

Options are a wasting asset, meaning the value of an asset (such as a car) tends to decline over time. The passage of time makes an option less valuable. That can be bad news for those who purchase options while being good news for those who sell them.

Potential for Total Loss

Options strategies run the gamut from high risk to low risk, but each strategy has the potential to be a total bust. Traders who purchase options are putting their capital on the line for the chance to make many times their money back, with the downside that they are likely to lose their entire investment.

Nothing Is Guaranteed

While selling options may be a safer strategy and more likely to succeed, even this approach can be subject to significant loss, with the potential to lose more than you gain.

Potential to Lose Way More Than You Earn

Traders who sell options can lose way more than they can possibly earn in any trade. For example, if you sell an option as insurance, you could lose much more than the money you received as an insurance premium. In this situation—and unless you have protected your downside risk by purchasing an option—you can lose many multiples of the premium that you expected to safely earn.

ARE OPTIONS TOO RISKY? YES AND NO

Using Options to Magnify and Reduce Risk

Ask a random person on the street what they know about options, and the first response you're likely to get is that they're risky. When Hollywood wants to show financial risk, they may turn to stocks, but when they want to show a poorly understood financial risk that threatens to blow up the markets, options fit the bill. This reputation is certainly well founded, but it's not the whole picture. Yes, options can be risky, but they can also be used to limit risk in several ways, such as hedging investments to reduce the overall risk of a portfolio. Like so many things in life, options trading can be relatively safe as long as you adhere to specific guidelines. That doesn't mean it's risk-free, of course, but it illustrates the point of legendary investor Warren Buffett who said, "Risk comes from not knowing what you're doing." So, it's useful to know the ways in which options can be used safely and the places where they can be quite risky.

HOW ARE OPTIONS RISKY?

The following characteristics can make options risky, but in some cases it's how you use—or misuse—an option that makes it risky.

Your Entire Investment Can Expire Worthless

For options that you purchase—as opposed to sell—you're putting your money on the line for the chance to multiply it many times. If the trade works out well, you can more than double your money and sometimes do so in weeks or months. The flip side is that your investment could expire worthless, leaving you with literally nothing. There's no question—it's a high-risk, high-potential-return trade. That's why many traders make options a relatively small part of their portfolio and fully understand the risk that their option may become worthless.

You Can Lose More Money Than You Could Ever Get Out of a Trade

For options that you sell—as opposed to buy—you get a cash payment up front but you make a promise that you'll buy or sell a stock in the future, if the stock or fund price reaches specific levels. If you sell the wrong option, it's entirely possible that you could lose many times the cash you've received. However, some of these kinds of strategies are the most popular, and if they're used judiciously, they can be an attractive way of generating income from options. In fact, you have ways to limit the risk on this type of trade, including ones that are popular with risk-averse investors.

Sensitivity to Asset Prices

Option prices are highly sensitive to the price of the underlying stock. If the stock moves a little, the stock option could well move 100%, 200%, or more, especially at certain points where the option becomes valuable. For traders, however, this volatility is an attractive feature of options, allowing you to make money quickly if you can find the right option. Of course, options trading is a zero-sum game, so somebody's win is somebody else's loss.

HOW CAN OPTIONS LIMIT RISK?

It's clear that options present risks, but the following features of options allow you to use them to limit risk.

Leveraged Exposure to a Stock

Options offer leveraged exposure to a stock. That is, you can put up a relatively small amount of money and make a significant profit if the stock moves in a favorable direction. This feature means that you can make a small bet on an option and enjoy profits that would require a much larger investment in the stock. If the stock is particularly risky and might decline a lot, you could lose a lot more money owning the stock than owning a much smaller position in the option that offers the same potential profit. So, purchasing an option can be a less risky way to enjoy the stock's price movement during a certain time with lower overall dollar risk.

Options May Surprise You

It may surprise some people to hear that you can use options to limit risk, given their reputation for being risky, but it's true. Options can limit your absolute dollar exposure to a given stock or fund, while offering the same upside potential or more.

Buy "Insurance" on a Stock or Investment Fund

Options also allow you to purchase "insurance" on a stock or an exchange-traded fund. This insurance acts as protection for your holding in case a stock falls, and it requires the person who sold you the option to buy your stock at a predetermined price. So, while your stock may fall, the option may become more valuable, offsetting most or even all your loss. By using options this way, you can proactively and intelligently limit certain risks in your portfolio.

Obtain Better Purchase Prices on Desirable Stocks

You can use the same strategy of selling options to get a better purchase price on stocks that you might otherwise like to buy, helping offset your price on the stock. You can repeat this strategy over and over and may not even need to purchase the stock, reducing your net purchase price still further. For many, it's a way to generate income, though imprudent traders may use it so frequently that it becomes risky to their portfolio.

Options Present No Surprises

While Hollywood may make it seem that options present unknowable risks, publicly traded option contracts are fully standardized, so all potential consequences are known before anyone places a trade. You know—or at least should know—the possible outcomes of trading specific options, including how much could be gained and how much is at stake. What you're really taking a bet on is how likely or unlikely a specific outcome is, for example, whether a stock hits a certain price in a certain time. If you miscalculate, the potential outcome—though not its magnitude—is already established. So, unlike other high-risk activities, where the range of potential risks may vary widely, the range of financial risk in options is known. None of this is to say that options are safe, but their risks can be mitigated by "knowing what you're doing."

IS OPTIONS TRADING FOR YOU?

Key Questions to Ask When Considering Options Trading

There's no question that options trading can be exciting—but is it the kind of exciting that you want? Options trading is not for everyone, so before you get started, you should think about whether it's actually right for you. This self-analysis includes looking at your own financial needs, your commitment to trading, your risk aversion, and any other factors that might clash with trading this high-risk security. Even if you discover that trading options is not really for you, or at least not right now, it can still be worthwhile to learn how it works and get intellectually comfortable with this glamorous side of the market. If you decide to come back to it, you'll be that much further ahead.

HOW TO DECIDE IF OPTIONS TRADING IS RIGHT FOR YOU

You'll want to look at several factors to see if options trading makes sense for you. Other individual considerations may also be more relevant in your situation.

Your Financial Needs

Trading options is close to gambling, even if it's gambling with an investing edge. If you're working with options, you must use only money that you do not need. There's a reasonable chance that you will lose some or all the funds you dedicate to options at the beginning, when you're learning how everything works and discovering the real risks firsthand. Given its risks, trading options is only for those who have no problem meeting the rent or mortgage payment, your child's tuition bills, and all the other expenses of modern life. In addition, you probably should have the rest of your financial life in order, including a growing retirement account and plenty of emergency cash on hand. If you need money—really *need* money—options are not for you. To put it another way, you don't have the money to gamble unless you're financially secure.

Experience

Options are not for the novice investor. To succeed in options, you need a strong background in stocks. You need to understand how they work, what moves their prices up and down, how to analyze them, what to look for in an investment, how to read financial statements, and . . . well, the list could go on and on. The investing world always offers something interesting to learn about. Of course, you don't need a doctorate in stock investing to succeed in options, but you need to feel comfortable that you know what you're doing with equities. If you don't have this knowledge and comfort, you'll be too prone to make errors with options, where they can be truly expensive. Even when you have deep stock knowledge, it's worthwhile to go slow with options so that you can develop your knowledge in this adjacent domain, especially when it comes to options' high volatility.

Time Commitment

Options can consume a lot of your time as you search for interesting trades and develop your fundamental knowledge of stocks that could be good options candidates. You may find options more rewarding if you can devote more time to them, but even those who devote a little bit of time may still find it worthwhile. For instance, while you might be investing mostly in stocks, you can layer on an options strategy or two, leveraging your existing stock knowledge. But you will need to keep an active eye on those options and manage them. Unlike a buy-and-hold stock portfolio, where you needn't spend time thinking about selling a position, with options you need to make active trading decisions, especially as an option's expiration date approaches. This active approach requires more thought and a thorough understanding of options pricing dynamics, at least if you want to make smart decisions. And if you don't have the time, don't sweat it—you can make plenty of money with stock investing with less work, especially if you're investing in funds.

Interest

Options are an exciting area of the market, where you can make (and lose) lots of money quickly. It can be intellectually interesting to analyze traders and what strategies they're using, and often the options world leads the rest of the market. But if you don't have an abiding interest in the area, it can be hard to sustain the drive to do the work needed to be successful. If you are interested, you can proceed at your own pace and let your interest drive your motivation to learn more. You'll never run out of things to learn in the investing world.

Risk Aversion

If you thought stocks were risky, options take the risk factor up a few more rungs. Not only can your option expire totally worthless, and you can be required to cough up money to buy stock, but options can be tremendously volatile. What was a nice gain at the start of the day may quickly turn into a loss by the end of the day, or vice versa. Even if the options roller coaster is working in your favor (i.e., going up), all that volatility can upset the stomach of risk-averse traders.

Plus, as mentioned before, if your risk aversion is not only temperamental but also due to financial need, options may not be your thing. Investors have plenty of good money to be made out in the stock market with less whiplash.

WHAT IF OPTIONS TRADING IS NOT RIGHT FOR YOU?

So, what if you discover that you're not cut out for options? That's fine. They require time, experience, interest, and plenty of surplus cash. It's not a combination that a lot of people have. If options do still hold some appeal, you should learn how they work. One of the hardest parts is simply understanding all the options dynamics, and once you have that mastered, you can come back later and be further along the path to trading, if that's what you want to do.

If options trading is not right for you, you have plenty of other easier, less time-consuming ways to make money. Find the ways that work for you.

Advice from Warren Buffett

Legendary investor Warren Buffett said, "There are no called strikes in investing." Buffett's words suggest that you get to pick when and how you invest in the market. If options aren't for you, find a type of investment that is.

A FOUNDATIONAL UNDERSTANDING OF INVESTING

What to Know Before You Trade Options

While you may be champing at the bit to get started trading options, you're still going to need to have the basics of investing down cold. These basics are an absolute "must have" if you're going to anticipate how stocks—and therefore, options—will perform over time.

A stock's price can be broken down into two key elements that determine what it's worth. First, a company's profits are the long-term driver of a stock's price. Earnings are often measured on a per-share basis—earnings per share—to provide a common basis for evaluation. Second, the earnings multiple is the amount that investors are willing to pay for a dollar of the company's earnings. Sometimes investors will pay a lot, while other times they won't pay much at all. One popular earnings multiple is the price-earnings ratio (or P/E ratio).

If you multiply the company's earnings per share by how much investors are willing to pay for each dollar of earnings, you get the stock price. So, evaluating how a stock will move is based on analyzing factors that affect its earnings and those that affect the earnings multiple.

A Fact Multiplied by an Emotion

A stock price is a combination of a fact (the company's earnings per share) multiplied by an emotion (how investors feel about the stock). In the short term, investors' emotions can dominate how stocks are priced, but over time, it's the earnings that move the stock.

WHAT AFFECTS A COMPANY'S EARNINGS?

A company's earnings are affected by its own performance and macroeconomic factors.

Company-Specific Factors

A company's ability to grow earnings depends on factors such as:

- **Sales growth:** Investors are looking for successful businesses that will increase their sales, and therefore profits, over time. In general, the faster, the better.
- **Margin expansion:** High margins (gross, operating, net) are signs of a healthy business. Higher-margin companies will grow their profits faster for the same level of sales growth.
- **Market opportunity:** A big potential market offers more upside, especially over time, than a small market. That is, a global market offers more potential gain than a domestic-only market.
- **Sustainable competitive advantage:** A company that has a competitive edge that it can keep for a long time is a more valuable business.
- **Strong balance sheet:** A company that has a strong balance sheet, including low debt, will tend to perform better than one that has significant financial issues.
- **The company's use of cash:** Stocks that pay dividends and companies that repurchase their own stock are more highly valued than those that don't.

This list could go on and on, and it's important to analyze the company's fundamental features so that you understand its strengths and weaknesses.

Macroeconomic Factors

Macroeconomic issues affect the business in direct and indirect ways:

- **Interest rates:** Lower rates make it cheaper for companies to borrow money to expand.
- **The state of the economy:** A growing economy helps drive corporate profits and spending growth that can move the economy forward for years.
- **Supply shocks:** A supply shock to an important commodity can hurt companies that depend on it directly and the wider economy.
- **Government intervention:** Government intervention to establish, defend, or curtail markets may affect the success of businesses.

Regardless of the company, it's impacted by the larger economic factors like those just described and many others.

VALUATION

New investors also need to understand how the market values companies and what factors lead to a strong valuation. In general, features that increase investors' optimism and confidence about the future success of the business drive a higher earnings multiple. If investors are confident about how a business will perform in the future, they're willing to value its earnings at a higher multiple today, driving its stock price higher.

In the short term, stock prices often follow valuation factors that may not have anything to do with the business:

- **Interest rates:** Interest rates are one of the most important factors influencing stock prices. Lower interest rates tend to raise asset prices, making them more attractive, compared to the risk-free return on cash. Higher rates tend to lower asset prices.
- **The stock's demand and supply:** Over short periods stocks may rise simply because there are not enough shares to go around, for example, with a hot new stock.
- **Momentum:** Stocks that have risen often go on rising, even if they're expensive on conventional valuation metrics such as a price-earnings ratio. The reverse is true, too—stocks that have lagged may keep on lagging until a "catalyst" comes along. But a surging market leads to "animal spirits," the risk-taking behavior that drives a stock up.
- **Unattractive "price action":** Many traders watch charts to predict future moves and rely on a variety of factors such as a stock's moving average prices. If a stock shows that it's about to "break out" or falls below a trend line, traders may increase buying or selling.
- **Investors' expectations:** Investors' expectations drive stock prices, and if a company doesn't deliver the high performance expected by investors, the stock could drop. The stock may also surge if the company delivers results that are above expectations or is able to consistently deliver a strong performance. But investors' optimism can drive up a stock even if the company is not yet earning any profits.

Understanding these valuation elements and where they're going can show where the stock may go and how much investors will pay for a dollar of earnings. Today's high earnings multiple may not persist tomorrow. A company may deliver excellent results—strong profit growth, for example—but if investors expected more, it won't matter. Or if interest rates rise, investors may have better alternatives for their money than stocks, pushing stock prices lower. Still, strongly performing companies tend to enjoy high earnings multiples for years and years.

THE IMPORTANCE OF UNDERSTANDING HOW INVESTING WORKS

This book advocates a fundamentals-based approach to trading options, that is, looking at issues directly related to the company's performance and valuation to inform trading decisions. These fundamental factors for stock performance underpin the direction a stock will move and therefore basic trading decisions as to which options strategy to use. But some traders—especially those focused on short-term price moves—look at technical factors such as a stock's recent price movements. Other traders look at both types of factors as well as the broader economic climate to help forecast stock moves. Regardless of your approach, find a way that works for your trading process. Understanding the factors driving stock prices is vital for options traders because they're making wagers on which direction a stock will move. You need some belief that's more informed than a fifty-fifty coin flip.

WHAT YOU'LL NEED TO TRADE OPTIONS

Key Things You'll Need to Start Trading

To get started trading options, you'll need a brokerage account with a broker that offers options trading. You'll also need to meet the broker's minimum account size for trading options, and it may be valuable, and perhaps necessary, at some brokerages to have a margin account, which allows you to borrow money to purchase stock. Finally, you'll need to have experience in the market, and the more you have, the better your chances of gaining approval to trade options.

QUALIFYING FOR OPTIONS APPROVAL

Most major online discount brokers offer options trading, but you'll have to qualify by answering a few questions from the broker. They will also ask you what your objective is with options, with goals such as income generation, hedging, and speculation. These goals align with the various options strategies. The broker also wants to evaluate your experience and knowledge of the market and then may approve you for one of several levels of options trading, which are based largely on their relative riskiness. If you don't have enough experience for the level you want, the broker may simply not approve you or may approve you for a lower level of trading, which may not include your desired strategies. If you say you have a relatively safe objective such as income generation, don't expect approval for the highest tiers, which include the riskiest and most complex strategies.

Typically brokers have four or five levels and they're associated with several options strategies, which could look something like the following:

Level 1: Covered calls, cash-secured puts

Level 2: Long calls, long puts, long straddles, long strangles

Level 3: Spreads, diagonal spreads

Level 4: Uncovered calls, uncovered puts, short straddles, short strangles

Don't get hung up on the strategy names, as these are covered in later chapters.

Each level of approval is cumulative, so if you have approval for Level 2 trading, you also have approval for Level 1 trading. Each broker will have its own classification for these options strategies, and what falls in Level 2 at one broker may count as a Level 1 strategy at another. If you're not approved for the level that you want at one brokerage, try getting approval at another brokerage, or call up customer support and see if they can help you get what you want. Sometimes it can be as simple as changing what your objective is in the brokerage's questionnaire.

Other Considerations When Opening an Options Account

As you're deciding which broker to use, you'll want to remember a few other things that could affect your experience, including costs, research, minimum account size, and the brokerage's sophistication, the last of which can improve your experience in small but important ways.

When it comes to costs, a typical brokerage might charge $0.65 per contract as a commission, but a new breed of investing apps and cutthroat competition have led to no-commission trading on options at a handful of places. However, free may not always be free if these investing apps offer worse pricing and trade execution than the services you need to pay for. Plus, these free brokerages may not offer additional features, such as research, that can help you make smarter decisions or at least give you some perspective on a stock.

In that same vein, research is a necessary component of options trading. You can't just fly blind in the market, and this book advocates using fundamental research that analyzes the business, the stock, the company's financials, and many other factors to make trading decisions—as opposed to technical research, which analyzes price movements to make decisions. Of course, you can do your own research, and only you are responsible for your trading decisions. But it can be helpful to work with a brokerage that offers some quality fundamental research, and some of the top brokerages offer it free of charge to customers. You can also subscribe to investment newsletters, some of which offer high-quality picks, to find attractive opportunities. However, be sure to check the track record of the analysts to see if they're doing a good job.

If you're looking to get started trading options, the good news is that many brokerages don't require a large minimum account balance or sometimes even any balance to do so. In many cases you might have to put up only the cost of a trade to start, and that may be as little as a few hundred dollars. However, for more advanced strategies, a brokerage may require a higher account minimum. Even with a couple thousand dollars in the account, if you end up making a few bad trades, you could quickly burn through that bankroll. Plus, such a small bankroll does not give you a lot of room to make many trades, and you may be able to have a maximum of only two or three trades on at any one point in time. Of course, you can start small, but working with a bigger bankroll, perhaps $20,000 or $25,000, gives you some room to maneuver.

For certain types of options strategies, ones where you may need to purchase the stock if the trade goes the wrong way, the brokerage may require you to have a margin account. A margin account requires at least $2,000 in equity—cash and marginable securities—if you want to borrow against it, and options positions generally do not count toward your marginable equity.

Starting a Brokerage Account

When setting up a brokerage account for options trading, be sure that it offers the key features you need. Don't focus on cost so much that it rules out selecting a brokerage with other features that will help you succeed.

More sophisticated brokerages can also offer you other advantages. They may offer better trade execution and pricing, but they also may allow you to use more advanced options strategies. Some brokerages may not offer all options strategies, typically limiting clients to a few basic strategies such as covered calls. More advanced outfits will offer a complete range of strategies and may offer analytical tools to help you calculate the payoffs. Sometimes the better brokers offer visual tools that literally show you how a trade could play out in various scenarios. So, be sure a potential brokerage partner offers the strategies you intend to use, or you'll need to find a new brokerage.

Chapter 2

The Fundamentals of Options

Strike prices, underlying stock, premiums, the Greeks, puts, and calls—the world of options has a lot of vocabulary that you'll need to master before you can begin to talk meaningfully about the good stuff such as options strategies and how to use options. Once you've nailed down the vocabulary, you can then cover the fundamentals of options themselves, including the two major types of options, what major factors affect options prices, and other things affecting the options market.

But once you learn the fundamentals of options, you'll be able to expand your options trading in a near-limitless variety, finding attractive strategies that can make you real money.

KEY NEED-TO-KNOW OPTIONS TERMS

Know Your Way Around the Options Lingo

While you may know key investing terms, those will only get you so far in the world of options. Here you'll need to master a whole new vocabulary—some of it even in Greek—to understand and describe how options work. It's important to understand this options vocabulary fluently because it forms the basis for this book's later discussions on options. You don't want to be held up by a definition and then need to run back and look it up. The discussions in the rest of the book will be returning to these terms over and over, so it's important that this material is locked in.

So an option is the right but not the obligation to purchase the stock or another asset. But how exactly does it all work? Well, for publicly traded options everything is standardized, so the structure of one option is effectively the same as any other. Here are the most important terms:

- **Underlying asset:** This is the stock (or fund or index) on which you're purchasing the option. The option entitles you to buy or sell only this one stock. In other words, you can't buy Microsoft options and exercise them for Apple stock. Sometimes the term *underlying stock* is shortened to *underlying* for simplicity.
- **Strike price:** This is one of the most important terms in the options world because it's the stock price where the option becomes valuable or worthless at expiration. An option's strike price says at what price the underlying stock may be bought or

sold. Every option has a strike price, and where it stands in relation to the price of the underlying stock determines how valuable the option ultimately is.

- **Premium:** The premium is the cost of the option, regardless of whether you are the buyer and you're paying it or you're the seller and you're receiving it. If the word *premium* reminds you of an insurance premium, that may be because options can function at times much like insurance. On the exchange and at your brokerage, an option's premium is quoted in terms of price per share instead of the total value of the contract. For example, an options chain, which reports the prices of all a stock's options, may list the premium at $1.30. However, the cost to purchase a single contract would be $130, or the premium × 1 contract × 100 shares per contract.

- **Expiration:** Every option has an expiration, the point in time when the option ceases to exist and the option "side bet" is settled between the option's buyer and seller. The expiration date is important because it clearly defines when the option—and all its various risks—is definitively settled and subsequently terminated.

- **Contract:** Options are traded in a unit called a contract. Each contract represents 100 shares of the underlying stock. In general, it's not possible to purchase, say, a half of a contract. You trade contracts in whole numbers only.

- **Exercise a contract:** A trader exercises an options contract, calling it into effect. If the contract entitles the option owner to purchase the stock at the strike price, the owner can exercise the contract and take delivery of the stock, provided they have the cash or margin capacity to do so. Only the buyer of a contract can exercise it, while the seller must make good on the contract.

Traders tend to exercise contracts as expiration nears, as the option's time value approaches zero.

- **The option Greeks:** These are a set of Greek letters that define the drivers of an option's price, and they help traders understand how an option will move. They are sometimes simply called "the Greeks."
- **Long and short:** The term *long* refers to whether you own the option, while the term *short* refers to whether you sold the option to open a position. For example, you're long $35 calls, if you own them. If you sold $55 puts to start a position that's still open, then you're short $55 puts.

These terms are your working vocabulary to describe the key elements of an option, and every option can be described in reference to them.

THE TWO TYPES OF OPTIONS

Beyond the previous fundamental terms, however, you need to know the two types of options:

- **Call option:** A call option offers the right, but not the obligation, to purchase the underlying stock at the strike price until expiration. When the stock price rises, the call option increases in value, and inversely, when the stock price falls, the call option declines in value. The buyer of the call option pays the premium to the seller.
- **Put option:** A put option offers the right, but not the obligation, to sell the underlying stock at the strike price until expiration.

When the stock price falls, the put option increases in value, and inversely, when the stock price rises, the put option declines in value. The buyer of the put option pays the premium to the seller.

You may already be familiar with call options since they are more widely known. Often when employees join a company, they are given a type of call option. If the company's stock goes up, the option is likely to gain in value. Depending on the strike price, the time to expiration, and ultimately the company's success, this type of call option—just like the kind on public exchanges—can become very valuable.

The put option is less well known, and it allows you to profit from the decline in a stock. While call options may get all the glory in Hollywood films, adept traders can make just as much money with put options.

Focus On the ABCs

These two types of options—the call and the put—are the basis for every options strategy. Every advanced options strategy is simply a combination of one or both basic types of options, allowing you to get the risk exposure you're looking to achieve.

The key point here is that regardless of which direction the stock is moving, options can help you play that move. Options can help you make money when the stock is bullish (moving upward) or bearish (moving downward). A well-crafted options strategy can even help you make money when the stock is moving sideways, without a clear upward or downward direction—and it's all based on these two types of options.

CALL OPTIONS: REWARDS AND RISKS

The Need-to-Know Info

Call options are one of the two major types of options, and they are a popular way to wager on a stock price rising and can generate substantial profit, if successful. But you can also use calls to generate income and otherwise wager on a stock remaining stagnant or even falling. This section runs through some specific examples to help with your comprehension.

Remember, a call option provides the right to purchase the underlying stock at the strike price until the option's expiration. The owner of a call has the right to purchase the stock at the strike price, while the person who has sold the call has the obligation to sell the stock at the strike price, if the option is exercised.

The price of a call option rises when the underlying stock rises, and it falls when the price of the underlying stock falls. When the option expires, the right to purchase the stock under the terms of the option contract expires with it, and buyer and seller have no further rights or obligations.

HOW CALL OPTIONS WORK

Call options are valuable—what traders call "in the money"—when the stock price is above the option's strike price. If the option reaches expiration and the stock price remains above the strike price, then the option will retain some value. Otherwise, the option will expire worthless, and the broker will wipe away the worthless security from traders' accounts on the next trading day.

For example, imagine Microsoft stock trading at $100 and a call option with a strike price of $95.

The value of a call option

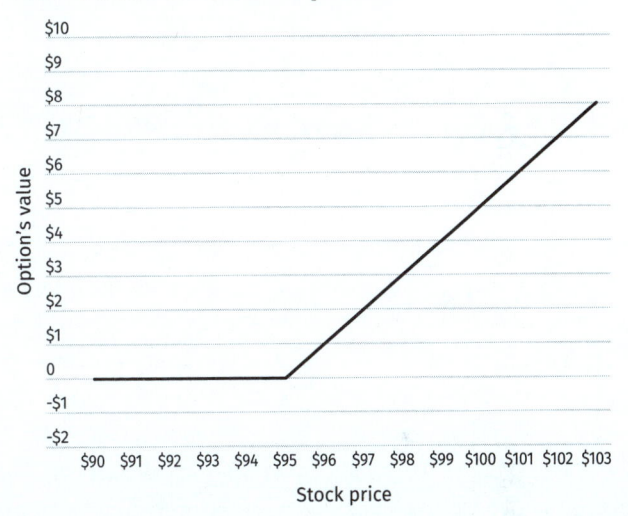

Currently this call option is in the money by $5. If the stock closed at $100 at the option's expiration, the option would be worth $5. The call allows the owner to purchase the stock for $95, and since the stock is trading at $100, the call is worth $5, or $100 – $95. If the stock rose to $102 at expiration, the option would be worth $7.

If the stock price fell below $95, the call would be "out of the money," and if the stock closed at $95 or below at the option's expiration, the option would be worthless. A trader is not generally interested in buying a stock for $95 that could otherwise be purchased for less than $95.

If the stock is above the call's strike price at expiration, the call retains some value. But generating a profitable options trade is not just a question of whether the option is in the money or not but also a question of the premium paid or received for that option. So, you could have an in-the-money option that is ultimately an unprofitable trade. In the example just described, if you had purchased the option for $6 and it was now worth $5, then you lost money.

THE PROFIT ON CALL OPTIONS

Whether an option trade is profitable depends on the relationship between the strike and stock prices, as well as what side of the trade you're on, whether buyer or seller, and the price you paid or received.

A call buyer profits when the stock price is above the strike price by more than the premium paid for the option. In the example in the previous section, if the stock is $100, the call's strike price is $95, and you paid $3 for the option, then the trade generated a profit of $2, ignoring trading costs. The stock must close expiration above the strike price for the call option to have any value at all.

A call seller profits when the premium received plus the strike price is more than the stock price at expiration. In the example just described, if the stock is $100, the call's strike price is $95, and you received $3 for the option, then the trade generated a loss of $2. However, at prices below $98—the $95 strike plus the $3 premium—the call is profitable for the seller. If the stock ends expiration below the $95 strike, the option expires worthless, and the seller keeps the entire premium.

Remember, options are priced in per-share amounts, so an option that is worth $5 really means that this option has a total value of $500, or $5 × 1 contract × 100 shares per contract.

The Option Value of Time

In this book's examples, you hear about the value of the option at expiration. For most of an option's life, however, it has an extra bit of value called time value that would make it worth more.

Whether you're the buyer or seller in this transaction, the breakeven point is the same—$98 per share of stock. This leads to a key point about options: The returns for the option buyer and seller are exactly opposite. If the call buyer makes $10 on the trade, then the call seller loses that same amount (again, ignoring transaction costs). So, one trader's loss is exactly another trader's gain. For call options, the buyer profits when the stock is above the breakeven point, while the seller profits when the stock is below the breakeven.

WHAT ARE THE REWARDS OF CALL OPTIONS?

Trading call options can be highly lucrative, and you can multiply your money many times or generate income. Calls can rise many times in value if the underlying stock continues to rise, and in fact, the profit potential is uncapped. In other words, there is no theoretical limit to what a call option could be worth. The call buyer can participate in this potential upside at the risk of losing the entire option premium. Calls expire worthless if the underlying stock falls below the strike price at expiration. By selling a call that may become less valuable or even worthless at expiration, the call seller generates a fixed cash premium with the hope that the stock will not rise or not rise too much. The potential loss to the call seller is uncapped.

Options can increase in price much faster than the underlying stock, making them attractive for traders who want to magnify the moves in the stock and rapidly increase potential gains.

Rewards and Risks of Calls

There are many other rewards and risks of calls, and the following are some examples:

- Call options can allow you to make many times your money if you purchase a call and the stock rises sufficiently before expiration.
- You can also use call options to generate cash by selling a call. The most a call seller can ever earn on a trade is the premium.
- A call buyer runs the risk of losing the entire investment if the stock does not finish above the strike price at expiration.
- In contrast, a call seller can lose not only the premium received but also much more, if the stock continues to rise. In theory, the potential losses could be infinite, though no stock has gone to infinity yet.

Call options have potential on both the buying and selling side for serious gains or losses—that's why it's so important to do research and understand what you're getting into before starting.

PUT OPTIONS: REWARDS AND RISKS

More Essential Information

Put options are the other major kind of option, and while they may be less well known, they're a popular way to wager on a stock price falling. Trading put options can also be highly lucrative, and they, too, can be used to generate income and wager on a stock remaining stagnant or even rising. This section will run through how they work.

Remember, a put option provides the right to sell the underlying stock at the strike price until the option's expiration. The owner of a put has the right to sell the stock at the strike price, while the person who has sold the put has the obligation to buy the stock at the strike price, if the option is exercised.

The price of a put option rises when the underlying stock falls, and conversely it falls when the price of the underlying stock rises. When the option expires, the right to sell the stock under the terms of the contract expires with it, and buyer and seller have no further rights or obligations.

HOW PUT OPTIONS WORK

Put options are valuable (or in the money) when the stock price is below the option's strike price. If the option reaches expiration and the stock price remains below the strike price, the option will retain some value. Otherwise, the option will expire worthless, and the broker will remove it from traders' accounts the day after expiration.

This similar but slightly different example from the last entry can illustrate how they work. For instance, imagine Microsoft stock trading at $100 and a put option with the strike price of $105.

The value of a put option

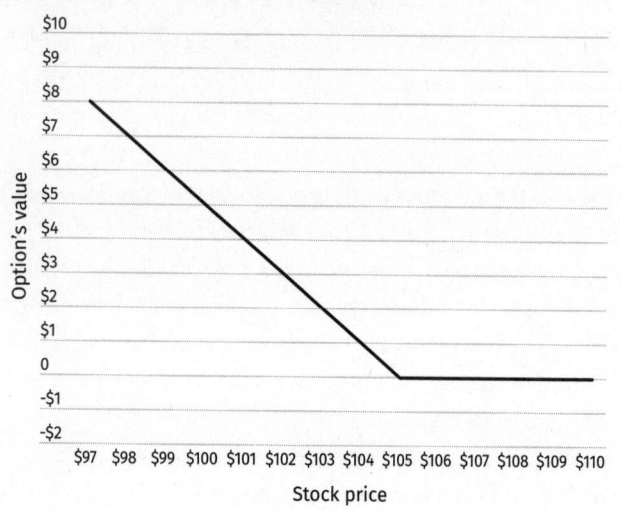

Currently this put option is in the money by $5. If the stock closed at $100 at expiration, the option would still be worth $5. The put allows the owner to sell the stock for $105, and since the stock is trading at $100, the put is worth $5, or $105 – $100. If the stock rose to $102 at expiration, the option would be worth $3. If the stock price rose above $105, the put would be out of the money. If the stock closed at $105 or above at the option's expiration, the put would be worthless.

So, if the stock is below the put's strike price at expiration, the put retains some value. But a profitable trade is not only a question of whether the put option is in the money but also a question of the premium paid or received. As with the call option, you could have an in-the-money put that is an unprofitable trade. In this example, if you had purchased the option for $7 and it was now worth $5, the trade was a net loser.

THE PROFIT ON PUT OPTIONS

Whether the put option trade is profitable depends on the relationship between the strike price and the stock price, whether you're the put buyer or seller, and how much you paid or received.

A put buyer profits when the stock price at expiration is below the strike price by more than the premium paid for the option. In the previous example, if the stock is $100, the put's strike price is $105, and you paid $3 for the option, the trade generated a profit of $2, not factoring in trading costs. The stock must close expiration below the strike price for the put option to have any value.

A put seller profits when the stock price is higher than the strike price minus the premium received. At stock prices above $102—the $105 strike minus the $3 premium—the put is profitable for the seller. In the example just described, if the stock is $100, the put's strike price is $105, and you received $3 for the option, then the trade generated a loss of $2. If the stock ends expiration above the $105 strike, the put expires worthless and the seller keeps the entire premium.

Options Lingo

Options are priced in what are called "per-share amounts." This means that any option worth $10 actually indicates that its total value is $1,000, or $10 x 1 contract x 100 shares per contract.

The breakeven point in this put transaction is the same for the buyer and seller, $102 per share of stock, if the premium was $3. As with call options, the return for the put buyer and seller are opposite. If the put buyer makes $5, then the put seller loses that same amount (still ignoring transaction costs). So, one trader's loss mirrors perfectly another trader's profit. For put options, however, the buyer profits when the stock is below the breakeven, while the seller profits when the stock is above the breakeven.

WHAT ARE THE REWARDS OF PUT OPTIONS?

Put options can also be highly lucrative, and savvy traders can make many times their initial investments or even use puts to generate income. Put options can multiply many times if the underlying stock continues to fall. However, unlike call options, the maximum value of a put is limited to the strike price. In other words, the put is most valuable when the stock goes to zero, at which point the put is worth the strike price. The put buyer can participate in this potential upside at the risk of losing the whole option premium. Puts expire worthless if the underlying stock rises above the strike price at expiration, which is good news for a put seller. By selling a put that may become less valuable, or even worthless, at expiration, a trader generates a cash premium with the belief that the stock will not fall or perhaps not fall too much. The potential loss to the put seller is capped at the strike price (i.e., the strike price × the number of contracts × 100 shares per contract), in the case of the underlying stock going to zero.

While puts differ in important respects from calls, both can rapidly magnify the price movement of the underlying stock, a particularly attractive feature to traders.

Rewards and Risks of Puts

There are many other rewards and risks of puts, and the following are some examples:

- Put options can allow you to make many times your money if the stock falls sufficiently before the option expires.
- You can also use put options to generate cash income by selling a put. The most the put seller can ever earn on the trade is the premium that was initially received.
- A put buyer risks losing the entire investment—the premium paid—if the stock does not finish below the strike price at expiration.
- Conversely, the put seller can lose not only the premium received but a whole lot more, if the stock continues to fall. In a worst-case scenario if the stock fell to zero, a put seller would have to still purchase the stock at the strike price.

You can make money with put options by buying and selling them, but have the potential to lose significant money too. So it's vital to do research and understand the risks and rewards before starting.

INTRINSIC VALUE VERSUS TIME VALUE

Two Key Parts of an Option's Price

An important concept in options pricing is called "moneyness," and it's central to thinking about whether an option will expire worthless or with some value. Moneyness is a measure of whether an option is "in the money" or "out of the money" and by how much.

- **In-the-money (ITM) options** are those that would retain some value if the option expired now. So, a call option is in the money if the stock price is above the strike price, and a put option is in the money if the stock price is below the strike price.
- **Out-of-the-money (OTM) options** are those that would be worthless if the option expired now. That is, a call option is out of the money if the stock price is below the strike price, and a put option is out of the money if the stock price is above the strike price.
- **At-the-money (ATM) options** are those where the stock is right at the strike price. These options, too, will expire worthless if the stock closes expiration there.

Traders also talk about deep-in-the-money options and deep-out-of-the-money options for those contracts where the stock price and strike price are very far apart. For a call option that is deep in the money, the premium would be relatively high as the stock price is much greater than the strike price, perhaps $10, $20, or more, depending on the stock price. For deep-out-of-the-money calls, the price may be $0.10 or $0.15, and the option may not even have a market, as no traders are willing to transact.

Importantly, an option is in the money or out of the money regardless of who owns it or whether it's a profitable trade. Its moneyness depends only on the relationship between the stock price and the strike price. Moneyness has nothing to do with whether you sold the option for more or less than you paid for it.

Weird Option Exercises

Even though an option is out of the money, you could still exercise it, though it would not make financial sense to do so. However, occasionally a trader may have a strategic reason to do so when the option is near the money.

THE TWO PARTS OF AN OPTION'S PRICE

Moneyness is also the basis for understanding the components that comprise the price of an option. The price of an option can be broken down into two major components, which can help you understand how the option is priced and how it might respond to various factors such as a change in the stock or the passage of time. The option premium is the combination of two elements:

Option premium = intrinsic value + time value

Intrinsic Value

Intrinsic value is how much of the premium is due to the stock being above or below the strike price. A call option has intrinsic value if the stock is above the strike price, and a put has intrinsic value if the stock is below the strike price.

Time Value

Time value—also known as extrinsic value—is the part of the premium that is attributed to its optionality, the potential that the option could increase in value, given its remaining lifetime and the stock's volatility. In short, it's whatever else that's not intrinsic value.

Here is an example to see how it works. Imagine Microsoft is trading at $100, and you can buy a call option with a $95 strike for $7. The option's intrinsic value is $5, or $100 minus the $95 strike. The option's time value is $2, or the $7 premium minus the intrinsic value of $5.

If this call expired right now, it would instantly become worth $5, or its intrinsic value. The option's $2 time value indicates how much investors are paying beyond the intrinsic worth for the potential upside during the option's remaining lifetime. An option's time value decays through the passage of time and particularly so in its last couple months of existence, so any remaining premium at expiration is comprised only of intrinsic value, if any, since no time value remains then.

For simplicity, when evaluating a trade's profitability, this book notes the option's price as if it were at expiration rather than making assumptions about an option's time value at some point during its lifetime. An option with substantial time to expiration is worth more than merely its intrinsic value, but you cannot accurately deduce what an option would be worth at any future moment without making assumptions. This approach simplifies things for clarity, and it's important to note that profitability is measured at expiration, at which point an option has no more time value.

PRICING DYNAMICS AND MONEYNESS

Understanding the makeup of an option's premium is important because it can help indicate movements in the option's price, particularly when the option nears expiration and time value is rapidly dwindling.

Are options with no intrinsic value worthless? No, not at all. But the option's expiration is the all-important deadline, and if the option does not finish in the money, it expires worthless. Options that have some chance of going in the money will retain more time value—on high-volatility stocks that could cross the strike price to gain intrinsic value, for example.

Options that are deep in the money start to perform like their underlying stocks, with price changes that look like the stock's. Even on options with a fair amount of time value remaining, if the intrinsic value drastically overwhelms the time value, the option's price movement starts to look like the stock's movement. As the option nears expiration, and with little time value remaining, the potential for an outsized gain is lessened and the option is more apt to be exercised.

On the other hand, options that are out of the money and have little chance of going in the money as expiration nears tend to wane quickly, as time value rapidly ticks down. The odds become lower and lower that the stock's volatility will bring the option into the money in the option's remaining lifetime. Deep-out-of-the-money options may well have lost all their value months before and will expire worthless.

But options that are close to the strike price may retain a surprising amount of time value even into their final days, especially for highly volatile stocks. That's because, with near-the-money options, the right stock move may send the option into the money even in the option's last days. While the absolute gain on the stock price might not be enormous, the percentage gain and the leverage offered by options may turn that price move into a massive winner. For example, an option priced at $0.50 that gets the right stock move the week of expiration might end up worth $3 or $4—a small absolute gain but a phenomenal gain in terms of the percentage.

WHAT AN OPTION IS WORTH

The Math Behind Options Pricing

So just how much is an option worth? In a real sense, the value of an option is whatever the market will pay for it, just as it is for any other asset. Traders are trying to estimate the value of an option based on what they know about the underlying stock or index and their expectations for how that underlying asset will perform over the life of the option. That assessment can change daily, and the price of an option can shift merely by how many buyers or sellers enter the market on a given day. But economists and market analysts have come up with ways to measure the theoretical value of an option, so this kind of theoretical basis may help underpin and support the market pricing of options.

WHAT MAKES UP AN OPTION'S PRICE?

Before touching on the theoretical work it's time to brainstorm a few ideas about what would move the price of an option. Put yourself in the shoes of someone looking to sell a call and get fair value from it. If you underprice that option, you risk losing out on some gains. But if you overprice it, another trader may not purchase it. So, what are the key factors that matter as you're pricing your option?

- **The potential price movement of the underlying asset:** Naturally, a big driver of an option's price is the price movement of the underlying asset and how much it might go up or down over the life of the option. A more volatile asset might go up more, meaning you want to charge more for the option today.

- **How long the option has until expiration:** If you want to sell an option that expires in the next five minutes, it will be next to worthless. In contrast, an option that expires in ten years may have substantial value because it could go up or down much more during that much longer time. That time has a real value to the owner of the option.
- **How likely the option is to be valuable at expiration:** Call options with a strike that is close to the stock price won't be worth as much as options where the strike is well below the stock price. In-the-money options have some built-in safety that you could charge more for.
- **What else you can invest in:** If you plan on selling an option, you're taking a certain risk to do so, and you expect a certain return for your risk. Well, what could you get instead—entirely risk-free—if you simply invested your money in a government-backed Treasury bill?

To sum up, an option seller is trying to price how much the underlying stock will move in the time of its existence, the intrinsic value of the option, and the alternative that could otherwise earn a risk-free return. Those are key potential risks that could affect the price of the option and therefore what you could sell it for.

THE BLACK-SCHOLES PRICING MODEL

Those factors just listed are some of the key inputs into the most popular option-pricing model—known as the Black-Scholes model—to calculate estimates of value of a European-style option (a type of option that can be exercised only on its expiration date). The equation was developed by American economist Fischer Black and Canadian economist Myron Scholes, and it was ultimately published in 1973. Later, American economist Robert Merton expanded on the model, which ultimately earned a Nobel Prize in 1997.

Like modern economics, the Black-Scholes model makes various assumptions to help it along, and those conditions may not always be in play. For example, the model assumes that the underlying stock does not pay a dividend and that trading options does not incur transaction costs. It also assumes that the volatility of the underlying asset is known by investors and that it's constant. Further assumptions include that the underlying asset's returns are normally distributed. All of this is to say, that its users are getting a stylized picture of an option's value, and that value can be a lot fuzzier in practice than it is in theory. Still, coming up with some idea of an option's value, even if imprecise, is far more useful than throwing your hands up and declaring, "Who knows?"

Black-Scholes—So What?

The ultimate point here is not to understand the math behind Black-Scholes—you absolutely don't need to—but rather to understand the dynamics that affect an option's price based on the key inputs in the Black-Scholes model and the bulleted list of key factors previously described. That is the key lesson, and it's what the model represents in mathematical terms. So, don't get hung up on the math here, but understand how the variables will move the price, even if not every Black-Scholes assumption holds.

By understanding these dynamics in basic terms, you'll walk away with a functional knowledge of how options are priced, and that's very valuable to you as a trader.

For example, it's useful to know that one of the key assumptions in the model is that the volatility of the underlying asset remains the same. But a stock's volatility may change due to predictable factors that analysts can spot if they're watching the business closely. Maybe a company introduces a hot new product that will suddenly drive demand and profits much higher. If a call option is being sold with a too-low estimate of the stock's future volatility, then the call will be underpriced. And the longer the call's time to expiration, the greater that underpricing will be. This potential mispricing in long-term options is one place where traders try to exploit some of the assumptions that go into pricing models. So, if you have a functional understanding of how the pricing dynamics work and understand potential weaknesses in the model, you can find potentially attractive places to profit.

Mispriced Long-Term Options

Long-term options can be an inefficient part of the options market. So, traders who can bring an informational edge—say, by understanding a company's financials and business prospects well—may find this area especially lucrative.

You also don't need to do the pricing math because several online calculators can do all the dirty work for you, leaving you more time to find the fundamental situations that offer real opportunities to profit.

KEY DRIVERS OF OPTIONS PRICES: THE GREEKS

Describing How Options Prices Move with Math

Options prices move for many reasons, and traders have ways to describe these price movements based on the inputs to the Black-Scholes options valuation model. For a change of one unit in each of the inputs, you can determine how much the value of the option should fluctuate. Each of these factors is denoted by a Greek letter, so traders call them "the Greeks." For example, you can determine how much a $1 movement in the underlying stock will affect the option's price, all else equal.

These measurements give you an idea of how sensitive the option price is to a change in the input. Therefore, you can see how quickly an option price can move if one of these Greeks changes. The key point is to understand which factors are working in your favor and which are not.

Caveat Calculator

An options calculator can help you determine the Greeks for a given stock and determine how an option might respond, but remember, it's only a guide. A good calculator allows you to adjust the inputs yourself to see how the factors affect the option price.

GET THEE TO THE GREEKS

This section runs through each of the five key Greeks, including what it is and how it affects an option's price.

- **Delta:** Delta measures the responsiveness of the option to a $1 change in the underlying stock price. Delta can range from 0 to 1 for calls (since they move directly with the stock) or –1 to 0 for puts (since they move inversely). For example, an option with a delta of 0.6 would move up by $0.60 if the stock price moved up by $1, or it would move down by $0.60 if the stock fell by $1. An option's delta can differ substantially depending on the distance between the stock price and the strike price. Deep-in-the-money options move nearly in lockstep with the stock price, while out-of-the-money options respond less to the underlying asset.
- **Gamma:** Gamma measures the change in delta, given a $1 move in the stock price. For example, if an option's gamma is 0.2 and its delta is 0.3, then a $1 increase in the stock should lead to delta changing to 0.5.
- **Theta:** Theta measures the responsiveness of the option to time. Options are wasting assets, and an option's time value constantly declines. So, the theta of an option tells you how much its value decays by the passage of a day. For example, an option with a theta of –0.03 will be worth $0.03 less tomorrow than today, all else equal. Theta is also called "time decay," and it's a key figure to pay attention to for options sellers, as time slowly helps increase their profit.
- **Vega:** Vega measures the change in an option's price due to changes in the implied volatility of the underlying stock. Specifically, vega measures the change in an option's price due to

a one percentage point change in the stock's implied volatility. Implied volatility is a measure of how volatile investors expect the stock to be during the option's lifetime. Stocks with higher implied volatility will have more expensive options, as traders want to be paid for potentially losing out on a stock's gains by selling the option. If an option has a vega of 0.04 and the implied volatility moves from 25% to 23%, or two percentage points, the option price declines by $0.08.

- **Rho:** Rho measures the responsiveness of an option's price to changes in the risk-free interest rate, usually by definition a Treasury bill that matches the option's expiration. Specifically, it measures the change in the option price to a one percentage point change in the risk-free rate. Unless the option is held for a long period or interest rates are notably volatile, this Greek does not impact pricing much and is not usually followed.

Additionally, traders may use other Greeks derived from these primary ones, depending on the strategy they're using.

WHY ARE THE GREEKS VALUABLE TO TRADERS?

Understanding the Greeks is not merely "nice to have" information. It's necessary to help traders make decisions, put on a trade, and know what they're paying for risk or how much they're being paid for it.

For example, theta is a key metric for those selling options, since they're looking to sell at a high price and repurchase the options at a lower price or let them expire worthless. Time is working in their favor, and theta measures how fast it's doing so. Theta changes over time and tends to increase as the option gets closer to expiration. In other words, an option's time value bleeds away faster as less time remains on the option.

Delta is used in hedging, and it indicates the ratio of the underlying stock to hedge, for traders using "delta-neutral" strategies to profit on changes in something other than the underlying. For example, for an option with a delta of 0.2, a trader would hedge 20% of the position. But delta can change over time, so you need to keep an eye on delta to maintain an optimum hedge. If you're trying to anticipate changes in delta, then you'll also want to know gamma.

Vega helps traders looking to profit on changes in a stock's implied volatility. When implied volatility is low, an option may be cheaper, meaning it may be a more attractive purchase if you expect the stock's volatility to increase in the future. Conversely, if implied volatility is high—say, a stock just soared—you might sell an option and take advantage of the higher volatility. If implied volatility comes back down later, then it could be an attractive time to close the position.

WHAT TO WATCH OUT FOR

The Greeks are only theoretical approximations of how the option will respond to a given change. Do not take them as gospel truth down to the second decimal place but rather as illustrative of the relationship between these factors and the option, with room to wiggle.

Also, it's important to note that these definitions have an "all else equal" caveat appended to them. These factors are all working at the same time to move an option's price. While theta decay is real and pares down the value of options over time, you can't just assume an option will be lower tomorrow than it is today if the underlying asset soars today or implied volatility spikes. What's key is knowing the relationship between the Greeks and an option's price so that you can make smart trading decisions, buying certain risks when they're cheap and selling them when they're pricey.

HOW OPTION PRICES MOVE

Options Pricing Is Anything but a Straight Line

Options pricing is a tricky subject. Several variables factor into pricing any option, and even though the stock may be the same distance from the strike price at different points in time, the option may be priced differently. Understanding these finer points in options pricing can help you develop a better intuitive understanding of how an option price will move.

OPTIONS MOVE NONLINEARLY

Options prices move nonlinearly—on a curve—as the various pricing factors play out in time, including the stock's movement relative to the strike price, time decay as an option approaches expiration, and changes in implied volatility, among others. For example, time decay does not occur as a straight-line decline in the option's time value until expiration. Instead, the rate of decay is impacted by how many days to expiration remain as well as how far the stock is from the strike price.

For simplicity, however, this book calculates the values of options strategies and examples at expiration, when a fully known and quantifiable price can be established. But at any point in its existence, an option is worth more than what it would be worth at the same stock price at expiration, since the option always has some time value right up until it expires. Because of this "extra" time value, a trade often realizes a higher profit if it's closed before expiration. So, you need to actively evaluate your options positions to realize the best reward for the risk.

TIME DECAY MOVES SLOWLY, THEN QUICKLY

Time decay affects options prices in different ways, depending on the time remaining to expiration and the moneyness of the specific option. Options with a long time until expiration will see theta decay affect the option's time value relatively little, as seen in the graph. But theta decay picks up speed noticeably in the last couple months of an option's life and then really accelerates in the last thirty days of its existence. So, options in their last weeks will see their time value plunging.

The effect of theta decay also depends significantly on how far the stock is from the strike price, either higher or lower. Theta is highest for options that are at or near the money, while theta declines as an option moves away from its strike price, either (deep) in the money or (deep) out of the money.

Theta decay over time

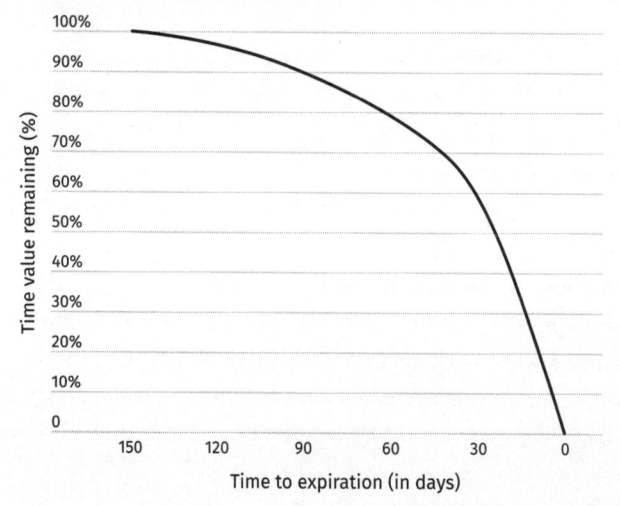

Deep-in-the-money options have proportionally less time value on them, as intrinsic value makes up most of the option's value. So, theta decay has a tiny impact on their price. It's a similar situation but in reverse for deep-out-of-the-money options, which are so far from being profitable that all that remains is a tiny bit of time value, and it ticks down slowly. Owners of these underwater options are paying so little for the time that they may be loath to part with the option for a pittance, and so they hold on, even if the odds are low that the option ever goes in the money.

It's a different situation with at- or near-the-money options. These options have a real possibility of being worth something at expiration, and even in the last days of existence, the option may go in the money if the stock moves favorably. So, at- or near-the-money options have the highest theta, as they have a large percentage of their total value comprised of time value.

HOW IMPLIED VOLATILITY AFFECTS PRICING

The effect of implied volatility on options prices differs based on the moneyness of the option as well as time to expiration. Volatility tends to affect out-of-the-money options the most, then at-the-money options, and finally in-the-money options, in percentage terms. An option whose price consists of a greater proportion of time value (i.e., out-of-the-money options and at-the-money options) moves more, percentage-wise, with a change in implied volatility. Options with proportionally more intrinsic value and less time value (i.e., in-the-money options) move less in response to changes in volatility.

The effect of implied volatility can differ depending on time to expiration. If implied volatility rises uniformly across expirations, it might affect the prices of far-term options more than near-term options, since far-term options offer more time for volatility to result in a wider range of prices. However, if a change in volatility is short-lived and long-term volatility remains mostly unchanged, only near-term expirations will be substantially affected. Implied volatility may not be uniform across expirations, as specific expirations experience higher levels due to anticipated events such as earnings. The combined effects of time and moneyness may see near-term, at-the-money options move significantly due to changes in implied volatility, as the option may go in the money if the stock moves favorably.

Volatility Rush and Crush

When implied volatility increases options prices, perhaps due to impending news or an earnings report, it's called a "volatility rush." When implied volatility subsides and causes options prices to fall, perhaps due to the lack of news or following an earnings report, it's called a "volatility crush."

WHAT DOES IT MEAN FOR OPTIONS TRADERS?

The pricing dynamics explained here mean that some trading strategies offer potentially extra good returns for the risk you're taking. Here are two strategies that may offer better risk-adjusted returns.

Far-Term Long Options Can Be Favorably Mispriced

Because theta decay works slowly on long-dated options, the price of far-term options can offer a good opportunity to multiply your money, and it's part of why this book focuses on a fundamentals-based approach to options. If you can identify a stock that's poised to appreciate significantly in the future, far-term options with a life of at least a year, though longer is better, may offer excellent value. On far-term options—even out-of-the-money options, where all value is time value—time decay works slowly at first, so the cost of time can be relatively low. Combine this advantage with an understanding of the company and what the stock could be worth in a year or two, and you can pick an attractive strike price that can multiply your money without paying a fortune for time.

Near-Term Short Options Can Be Favorably Priced

If far-term options can be attractively priced for option buyers, near-term options can be attractive for sellers. Time value is working in the favor of sellers, not only ticking down the value of options but ticking it down at a higher rate in the last weeks of the option's life. So, the yield per day is higher in an option's last days—a clear boon for the option seller. Selling a series of one-month calls on the same stock at the same strike price, assuming the stock is flat, tends to yield more than selling the equivalent far-term option once. That is, you could sell a one-month option each of the next two months and earn more than selling the two-month option at the same strike today.

Advanced traders have even more ways to take advantage of the nuances of options pricing and carve out lower-risk profits.

PUT-CALL PARITY

The Key Principle Keeping Options Markets Efficient

Put-call parity is an important concept in the options world, and it gets to the very structure of how options function, but it has a complex basis. The concept of put-call parity says that the price of a call implies a fair price for a put option with the same underlying asset, the same strike price, the same expiration, and all else equal. It applies to European-style options, which cannot be exercised before expiration. If this pricing relationship of matched calls and puts is violated, it indicates some inefficiency in the market that could be exploited for a risk-free profit via arbitrage. Arbitrage is the buying and selling of an asset in different markets to exploit a pricing difference in the markets, making it essentially a return without risk. In general, though, the options market is efficient, and few opportunities exist for risk-free gains.

THE FORMULA FOR PUT-CALL PARITY

To understand what put-call parity means for options pricing, consider the mathematical formula for it, assuming a non-dividend-paying stock:

$C + PV(k) = P + S$

C: The price of the call option

PV(k): The present value of the strike price discounted at the risk-free rate

P: The price of the put option

S: The share price of the underlying asset

This formula says that the price of a call option plus the present value of the call's strike price equals the price of a put option with the same strike price plus the share price of the asset.

Now consider an example to see how it works and what it implies about the put price for a given call price. In this example, take a non-dividend-paying stock with a price of $20 and a $22.50 call with a price of $1.10 that expires in six months. Assume a risk-free rate of 4%. How much should the $22.50 put option be worth here?

$$\$1.10 + \$22.06 = P + \$20$$

The present value of the strike is calculated as $22.50 divided by the sum of 1 + (4% × Years). Solving for P, the fair price for the put option is $3.16.

Put-call parity holds up well in practice, though transaction and borrowing costs may affect the real-world pricing somewhat. This result is another way of saying that the options market is efficient and that individuals do not have many opportunities for substantial risk-free profits using arbitrage.

HOW DIVIDENDS AFFECT PUT-CALL PARITY

If you look at the options pricing on a dividend stock, you might think something is off with put-call parity. The calls look too cheap, while the puts look too expensive, for a given strike price and expiration.

As an example, look at Altria, a stock with a notably high dividend of $4.08 per year. In this example the stock trades for $50, and a $52.50 call for about a year out trades at $1.98. Use a risk-free rate of 4%. Assuming for a moment that the stock didn't pay a dividend, how much should a put at a similar strike price trade for using the formula?

$$\$1.98 + \$50.48 = P + \$52.50$$

The formula suggests the put should be trading for –$0.04, or more than free! This result makes no sense, suggesting that the call at $1.98 is trading much cheaper than it should. In actuality, the Altria put traded for $6.02, reflecting primarily the fact that the stock paid a significant dividend and that this is an American-style option, which allows exercise before expiration. The real-world option price factors in the dividend payout, which reduces the stock price at each quarterly distribution. A modified Black-Scholes formula for put-call parity corrects for the issue of dividend-paying stocks.

Watch Out for Dividends!

Dividends affect options prices. The takeaway for you is to pay attention to pricing with dividend stocks, as calls will look too cheap and puts will look too pricey, so you may not be getting what you think.

The dividend also has a real effect on trading dynamics. Call options are more likely to be exercised just before the stock goes ex-dividend (the day the dividend is subtracted from the stock price), while put options are more likely to be exercised on the ex-dividend day or after, since the stock price is lower, reflecting the dividend adjustment.

OTHER CONCLUSIONS
OF PUT-CALL PARITY

Put-call parity also implies that every stock and basic options position can be reformulated as a combination of a stock and/or other options strategies. In other words, you can synthesize another strategy from various parts, like some Dr. Frankenstein of options. The put-call parity formula can be rearranged mathematically to show the following relationships:

- A long call is equivalent to owning the stock plus a long put
- A short call is equivalent to being short the stock plus a short put
- A long put is equivalent to being short the stock plus a long call
- A short put is equivalent to being long the stock plus a short call
- Being long stock is equivalent to owning a long call plus a short put
- Being short stock is equivalent to a short call plus a long put

Spend a moment to think about what some of these equations are saying. Take the formula for being long stock, which consists of buying a call and selling a put. This strategy is also known as a synthetic long, and it's covered later. For now, consider that by gaining exposure to these pieces of a stock's risk profile via options at the same strike price and same expiration, you're replicating the performance of the stock. If the stock rises, the call rises, whereas if the stock falls, the short put increases in value, hurting your position. It's a similar situation for shorting stock, using a short call and a long put to synthesize the performance of shorting the stock, and it's called a synthetic short.

These formulas derived from the original put-call parity equation show the equivalencies you can use to bring options pricing in line if it deviates from that of the stock. Using the synthetic long equivalency, for example, the net price of a long call and a short put should equal the difference between the strike price and the stock price. If it doesn't, you can trade the stock, its call, and its puts until there's no more risk-free profit here.

KEY OPTIONS STYLES

American or European?

Options fall into two other broad styles that are worth exploring further, so that you understand what's out there, though it may have little effect on your actual trading. Most options that you see out in the wild fall into one of two broad categories: **(1) American-style options:** An American option can be exercised at any point before the expiration date, and **(2) European-style options:** A European option can be exercised only at the expiration date.

Which style you encounter most frequently depends a lot on the underlying asset. Options on stocks are typically American, so if you're trading stock options, you might get an early exercise from time to time, depending on the exact circumstances. In contrast, most index options traded in the United States are European-style. Many futures options traded on the Chicago Mercantile Exchange, a huge derivatives market, are European-style.

In most circumstances, you don't need to pay too much attention to the style of your option. However, when the underlying asset pays a substantial dividend, it may sometimes be advantageous for the owner of an American-style call option to exercise it early and collect the dividend. Early exercise would make sense on the day before the stock goes ex-dividend if the dividend is greater than the remaining time value on the option. (The ex-dividend day is the first day the stock trades without the dividend.) Deep-in-the-money calls are especially prone to this type of early exercise, as most of their price is comprised of intrinsic value and very little is time value. Of course, exercising an option early to capture the dividend will not be a concern for European-style options.

Remember, the style differences are about when the option can be exercised, not about when you can buy and sell the option. You can always close your position regardless of which option style you have. Importantly, if you do not want to be subject to exercise, you can simply close your short options position—whether American-style or European-style—before expiration or before time value ticks down to nothing.

Moreover, the distinction between American-style and European-style options has nothing to do with what parts of the world they're traded. Both styles may be traded wherever options are traded, and both styles trade in the United States, though they're usually limited to certain types of securities. In other words, options on stocks are usually American-style, while futures options on the Chicago Mercantile Exchange, for example, are usually European-style.

WHEN DO THESE OPTION STYLES EXPIRE?

Because of their differing exercise conditions, these two styles of options also have differing expiration schedules. Standard monthly American-style options expire on the third Saturday of each month, and they stop trading at the end of the market day on the Friday before. In contrast, standard monthly European-style options expire on the third Friday of each month, and they stop trading at the end of the market day on the Thursday before.

Now the highest-volume stocks on the exchange also have weekly expirations, with an expiration on Saturday, while trading stops the day before. Some of the most popular stocks may soon have daily expirations as well, rapidly increasing the pace of options expiration for a select few stocks.

ZERO-DAY OPTIONS

Zero-day options are options that are literally on their last day of existence, and are sometimes known as ODTE, short for 0 days to expiration. At some point every option will become a zero-day option, but exchanges have also created daily index options that exist for just one day and then expire. These options cover a few exchange-traded funds based on major stock indexes such as the S&P 500 and the Nasdaq-100. These types of options trades have become popular in recent years, especially among individual traders, but they're tremendously risky.

Zero-Day May Mean Zero Pay

Risk-seeking traders see zero-day options as an opportunity to quickly multiply their money by the end of the day, though they're apt to expire worthless. Zero-day options are about "guessing right" rather than using an investment thesis to invest intelligently.

Zero-day options appeal to traders because of their explosive potential. Pick the right option, especially those with a strike price near the stock price, guess which way the underlying's price will move, and you could make many times your money in hours. With these options, you're paying little for the time value of options, so those with strike prices that are close to the underlying's price may pay little for the option. If the stock or index swings favorably that day and you guess right, you could win a lot. For example, imagine a slightly out-of-the-money call that trades for $0.25 at the start of trading on Friday morning. If the stock finishes the day at $1 above the strike price, suddenly that $0.25 option is worth $1. This explosive potential and a quick payoff have made zero-day options a fast-growing part of the options market, even though it's much like gambling and fraught with risk.

MORE OPTION STYLES

While you're likely to come upon only American and European options, those who run further afield may find some other types out there:

- **Bermudan option:** This style of option splits the difference between the American and European styles, allowing the owner to exercise the option early at a few predetermined points of time.
- **Evergreen option:** The evergreen option style requires the option holder to preset a time before exercising the option and can be applied to both American and European styles of options.
- **Binary option:** A binary option differs from the standard American- or European-style options. With a binary option, you're betting on one of two outcomes that are mutually exclusive, and the contract is settled in a short period, often in a single day. For example, a binary option may ask, "Will the S&P 500 close above 5,500 today?" You pick a side, and often receive a fixed payout, typically $100, if you're correct, or you lose everything if you're wrong. The pricing of these wagers updates dynamically

throughout the day so that lower-probability events will receive higher payouts if they come to fruition.

While other option styles are out there, you need to pay attention to American- and European-style options because they're the most prevalent and are offered on the most commonly traded products such as stocks, ETFs, index options, and others.

HOW ARE OPTIONS TAXED?

The Ins and Outs of Tax Rules

The tax treatment for options is not always straightforward. In fact, the tax rules can change, depending on whether you purchased or sold the option, how long you held it, and whether it's a simple "single-leg" trade or a more complex "multi-leg" trade. This segment reviews tax issues for investors working with publicly traded options on stocks and ETFs.

TAXATION ON SINGLE-LEG TRADES

The tax treatment on single-leg trades is not always straightforward, so it's key to know a few facts about the trade.

Single-Leg Long Options

If you purchased an option and then sold it or it expired, the tax treatment is simple:

- If you sold the option, your holding period determines whether the option is taxed at favorable long-term capital gains rates. You'll get these rates—currently 0%, 15%, or 20%, depending on overall income—if you held the option for more than a year. If you held the option for less than a year, as most options are, you'll be taxed at ordinary income rates, which are typically higher.
- If you purchased the option and it expires, it receives the same tax treatment as if it had been sold. If the holding period was more than a year, more advantageous long-term tax rates are used. If not, ordinary income tax rates are used.

If you exercise the option, however, the situation is treated differently:

- If you exercise a call option, the purchase price is added to the cost basis of the stock you acquire. You won't generate a tax liability when you exercise the option, and later, when you sell the stock, the capital gains tax rate is determined based on your holding period. If you hold the stock for a year or longer, you can take advantage of lower long-term capital gains tax rates.
- If you exercise a put option, the option's cost is deducted from the proceeds of the stock sale to figure your overall proceeds. The stock's holding period before the option exercise determines how the capital gain is treated.

Work the Options Tax Rules

The tax rules for exercising options may allow you to transform what would otherwise be short-term options gains into long-term gains that are taxed more favorably. It could make sense to consider whether these rules help you reduce your tax burden.

Single-Leg Short Options

If you sold a call or put option and repurchased it to close the position or the option expires, it's taxed as follows:

- If you close a short call or put option—one you wrote—it's always treated as a short-term gain or loss regardless of your holding period.

- If a call or put that you've written expires, it's considered a short-term capital gain.

  If an option you've written is exercised, it's treated as follows:

- If a short call has been exercised against you, then the option premium is added to the proceeds of the sale to determine your overall proceeds from the transaction. The holding period for the stock is what determines whether the gain or loss from the transaction is treated as short term or long term.
- If a short put has been exercised against you, subtract the option premium from the stock's cost basis to find the new tax basis. You won't generate tax when the option is exercised, and your holding period on the stock decides whether the capital gain or loss is short term or long term. Your holding period on the stock begins when you take delivery of the stock.

TAXATION ON MULTI-LEGGED AND HEDGED TRADES

Multi-leg options trades—those with two or more components—and hedged stock-and-option trades (such as covered calls) have still different tax treatments. With these more complicated types of trades, the tax rules try to keep you from realizing losses on one side of a multipart trade before you realize offsetting gains on another side. You can deduct a realized loss on one side of the trade only for the amount that exceeds an unrealized gain on another leg. If you're unable to write off the loss in the current tax year, you'll be able to claim it in the subsequent tax year. It's what the IRS calls restricted loss deferral. This rule is a real mouthful, so it may make more sense with an example.

Imagine you made a two-part trade, and you closed one leg for a $10,000 loss while the other leg remains open and has a $7,000 unrealized profit. You cannot claim the full $10,000 loss this year unless and until you realize the $7,000 profit on the other leg of the trade. However, you can still claim the loss above the unrealized gain, or $3,000, which is the $10,000 loss minus the $7,000 gain. When you close the profitable leg, you can claim the remainder of the loss on your taxes to offset the gain. The unrecognized gain is figured at fair market value on the final business day of the year.

Covered Calls

A covered call involves selling calls while owning the underlying stock. Covered calls are treated specially, and this treatment may help you legally avoid the loss-deferral rules explained previously. The covered-call trade must meet two major conditions to qualify: The option must not be deep in the money and the call must have an expiration of more than thirty days.

If the option doesn't meet the qualifications, then it will be subject to the loss-deferral rules. These special rules allow you to realize a loss on the call without having to close the related stock position. That's a real benefit if you have a significant unrealized gain in the stock that might be subject to tax if the stock had to be sold to claim the loss on the option.

Covered calls may also have another special tax treatment. If you set up a qualified covered call using a strike price that is below the stock price, a loss on the option leg is treated as a long-term capital loss if the sale of the stock would be treated as a long-term loss. When factoring the stock's holding period, however, don't include any time period since the call option had been sold.

OPTIONS ARE STILL SUBJECT TO THE WASH-SALE RULE

Options traders must still abide by the wash-sale rule, which limits when you can claim a loss on a trade. A wash sale is when you sell an asset such as a stock or option at a loss but have purchased the same asset or one that's nearly identical in a thirty-day period before or after that sale. The upshot: You won't be able to claim a tax loss on a wash sale. To claim the loss, you will need to sell out of the position and not repurchase it for at least thirty days. Even if a wash-sale loss is disallowed on a tax return, you can claim the loss in a future year if you clear the wash sale.

Chapter 3

How to Trade Options

This book approaches options trading as an extension of stock investing. With this approach, you can use an options strategy based on your fundamental stock analysis rather than just guessing at short-term moves. A fundamental analysis—understanding business performance, the stock's valuation, the company's competitive position, and so on—informs your view of how the stock may perform. Then you select an options strategy that matches this view. This approach contrasts to that of many traders, who use technical analysis to decide when to buy or sell. Technical analysis relies on analyzing the stock's price movements to see how it might move in the future.

In the short term, a stock price can go anywhere. However, over a longer term, a stock follows the company's fundamentals, so trading decisions should be based on those fundamentals. This knowledge edge and a longer-term perspective can be highly valuable advantages when trading options.

DEVELOPING AN INVESTMENT THESIS

Step One Is Knowing the Underlying Stock

To develop an investment thesis, you want to understand where the stock is going and how fast it might get there. Getting a read on those two variables can help you decide which options strategy makes the most sense. By doing this fundamental work, you'll be confident in where the stock moves and which options strategies will work best. If you don't have some idea where the stock is likely to go, you're just making stabs in the dark.

ANALYZE THE COMPANY

When doing a fundamental analysis, you want to develop a broad perspective of where the company is going by answering several questions. You don't need to know every little detail, but you do need to understand whether the company is likely to thrive and which direction the stock is likely to move.

Operational

These questions surround the business itself, including its products and competitive position:

- How is the company positioned relative to its peers? Is it a new company or an established cash cow? Is it a leader or second-tier player?

- Are the company's products well regarded and do they command higher prices in the market?
- Does the company have a sustainable competitive advantage, especially one that can last decades?
- Have the company's margins held up over time, or do they indicate a deteriorating business?
- What are the competitive threats on the horizon? Could an unforeseen development derail the business?

Operational factors such as these help you understand how the company may thrive, tread water, or even fail.

Financial

These questions surround how the business is financed and whether that's a strength or weakness:

- What is the financial position of the company—is it heavily indebted or does it have a lot of cash?
- What do the key financial ratios of the company tell you about its financial position? Debt to equity? Debt to EBITDA (earnings before interest, taxes, depreciation, and amortization)? Return on equity?
- What does the return on invested capital say about the company's competitive position? Has that ratio been rising or falling?
- Has the company used its cash smartly or has it blown a lot of money on poor acquisitions?
- Has the company repurchased stock and done so smartly?

These financial factors help you understand how well the company is using its cash and whether it's trying to drive returns for investors.

Valuation

These questions surround how the market values the stock:

- Does the market award the stock a high or low valuation on key measures such as price to earnings and enterprise value to EBITDA?
- Is the valuation high or low relative to this company's history?
- Are insiders buying stock in significant amounts, suggesting the stock price may be low, or are they selling any stock they receive as fast as they can?
- Is the stock price high, low, or somewhere in the middle, relative to its recent history?
- What is the fair value for the stock?

These lists are not exhaustive, but they offer the type of questions that you want to ask to get a good analysis of the business and the stock. Doing the fundamental analysis can take time, but you'll need this foundational knowledge to trade confidently. If you don't want to do this work yourself, subscribe to an investing or research service that provides reports on the stocks you need.

Brokers with Free Research

Some of the better brokers offer access to their in-house research or that of respected outlets such as Morningstar. These reports can jump-start your analysis and get you in the game faster and without too much cost.

DETERMINE WHERE THE STOCK IS GOING

Your fundamental analysis provides the backdrop for concluding where the stock will go over time. A company with a sustainable competitive advantage, consistently strong margins, and a high return on invested capital over many years can likely continue to thrive. Combine those features with a cheap or fairly priced stock and you might conclude that the stock will be higher in the next year or two. In contrast, a company with trouble holding its margins, problems growing consistently, or weak return on invested capital may be headed lower over time.

You'll want to develop some estimate of a stock's fair value using valuation techniques such as analyzing comparable stocks or performing a discounted cash flow analysis, both of which take substantial further work. Many research services provide their estimate of a stock's fair value, and while you'll want to take them with a grain of salt, they can give you a starting place. You'll want to understand the assumptions built into the estimate and whether they're reasonable, and your fundamental analysis helps here.

One gauge to how a stock may perform is how it has performed in the past. Of course, past performance is no guarantee of future performance, but good companies tend to keep on winning. These companies have competitive advantages that allow them to earn above-average profits and management teams that do smart things with those profits. You'll see those features evidenced in a stock chart that rises over time. The stock charts of companies with poor management teams and no advantages may continue to decline just as they have in the past. This visual analysis augments the fundamental work to give you a sense of where a stock could go.

You'll also want to consider how fast the stock can grow and the level of annual returns you might expect. High-growth stocks could return 25%–30% a year for many years. In contrast, an average well-run business might be able to deliver 8%–12% returns. Other growth stocks may deliver returns that fall somewhere in between. To see what a stock might do in the future, look at its annual performance over longer periods, such as five or ten years. This annualized information is available on public finance sites and at elite brokers, though you can run the numbers yourself.

Both the fundamental analysis and your expectations for the stock's future performance will help you determine which options strategy should work well for your situation.

FINDING THE RIGHT OPTIONS STRATEGY

The Right Strategy Can Lead to Huge Gains

You have your investment thesis and an expectation about where the stock should go, so now it's time to overlay an options strategy. It's vital to find a strategy that fits well with how you expect the stock to perform. If you think the stock will rise from $100 to $120 over the next six months, find an options strategy that profits on that move. The more your options strategy is aligned with the facts, the more money you're likely to make.

KNOW THE AVAILABLE OPTIONS STRATEGIES

It's important to know the options strategies that you have at hand for a given trading setup. These strategies are your available tools, and you want to be able to easily identify the strategies that work for the stock's situation. The basic strategies are found in the next chapter, and more advanced strategies are in the later chapters of the book. While you may prefer to specialize in certain areas, it's valuable to be familiar with all key strategies so that you have more choices available to you.

SELECT AN APPROPRIATE
OPTIONS STRATEGY

You can make money in different ways from a given setup, so carefully consider your expectations for the stock, the profit potential of various strategies, and your comfort level with using a strategy, given its risks. For example, some traders may simply not be comfortable going long because of the potential total loss of premium that's at stake. Other traders may be uncomfortable selling calls because of the potential risk involved there.

It can be useful to work through several questions about an options strategy to see if it's appropriate:

- If my investment thesis is right, what is the profit potential of this strategy?
- If my thesis is only partially right, how much money could I make or lose?
- How much money would I reasonably lose if my thesis is completely wrong?
- Am I willing to take the risk for the potential upside? Am I getting paid enough?
- What other options strategies overlay well with my expectations for the stock?
- Is there another strategy that delivers a better return for the risk I'm willing to take?
- Can I give this strategy a better return for the risk if I adjust the strike prices?

Play-Test Your Trades

It's valuable to game out the possibilities of a strategy to figure the risks and rewards and to get comfortable with a range of outcomes. As you develop your skills, you'll be more confident about your preferred strategies and how to set them up for the risk you're willing to take.

A PRACTICAL EXAMPLE

Consider how you could set up a trade with different strategies. Imagine Stock LMNO is trading for $100, you estimate it's worth $120 based on your analysis, and the stock isn't paying a dividend. You could set up the following strategies:

A long call: A $100 call is available for six months at a cost of $8. The option begins to break even at $108, so the stock needs to move up 8% before the trade even starts to make money. If the stock reaches $120 at expiration, the long call will be worth $20, netting you a profit of $12 per contract. However, if the stock is below $100, the option will expire completely worthless. At a stock price between $100 and $108 at expiration, the option will retain some value, but you'll lose overall.

A short put: A $100 put is available for six months with a premium of $8. You get this money up front and then are obligated to purchase the stock if it closes below $100 at expiration. If the stock closes above $100 at expiration, you keep the entire premium. If the stock closes between $92 and $100, then you have made a partial profit. And if the stock falls below $92 at expiration, you will be out more money than the $8 premium received.

It's possible to break these strategies down further.

The long call: This strategy works well when the stock has a lot of upside. If the stock runs to $120 or more, you get to keep all the extra profit. So, the long call offers an open-ended upside. However, it can take a substantial stock movement to reach the option's breakeven price, and you run the risk of losing the entire premium if the stock falls below $100. If you're only partially right—say, the stock rises to $105—you'll be out a net $3 per contract.

The short put: This strategy works well if you're looking to take less risk because the stock only must stay above $100 at expiration for you to collect the premium. If the stock is worth $120, a short put could be a good way to generate income with lower risk. Even if the stock only reaches $105 or $108, you keep the whole premium. As the put writer, you'll be obligated to purchase the stock at $100 if it's below that level at expiration. If the stock is worth $120, it's not so bad if you buy it at a net $92 (the $100 strike minus the $8 premium).

You'll need to estimate the profit potential and the strategy that you want to use given your expectations for the stock's performance. But you can further calibrate these strategies by changing the strike prices to adjust their risk and return, giving them a better risk-reward ratio.

LEARN TO READ THE OPTIONS CHAIN

Find the Trading Info You Need on the Chain

You've found the options strategy you want to use—now it's time to find some prices on it. Finding an option's price is not quite as simple as finding a stock's price. Brokers and public finance sites such as *Yahoo! Finance* and *Google Finance* offer an entire array of options prices called an options chain. You need to be able to effectively read the options chain to get the pricing for the options that you're interested in and to understand which options are available to trade. The chain also helps you compare prices on different strikes and expirations to see if a different option looks more attractive.

WHAT IS AN OPTIONS CHAIN?

An options chain is valuable because it provides you a lot of information in a quick although not-always-easy-to-read format. The options chain shown provides information such as the following:

- The monthly expirations available for a specific stock
- The available strike prices
- The option's symbol for each strike price and expiration
- The last price for the option
- The bid and ask prices for each option
- The open interest (OI) in a specific option
- The current day's trading volume

That's a lot of information presented in a dense chart, and it can be easy for newer options traders to be overwhelmed by the details. Worse, they could make errors and confuse details—for example, the last price on a put instead of a call—leading to significant problems, including inputting the wrong order.

The following is an example of an options chain for call options on GameStop.

Strike	⌐Bid	⌐Ask	Last	Change	Volume	OI
Oct. 18, 2024 3 days						⌄
Oct. 25, 2024 (W) 10 days						⌄
Nov. 01, 2024 (W) 17 days						⌄
Nov. 08, 2024 (W) 24 days						⌄
Nov. 15, 2024 31 days						⌃
16.00	5.30	5.80	5.33	-0.24	0	0
17.00	3.65	5.00	4.24	-0.41	0	0
18.00	3.45	4.00	3.92	+0.09	0	287
19.00	2.99	3.15	3.13	+0.01	0	86
20.00	2.38	2.66	2.49	-0.01	0	4,623
21.00	1.90	2.17	1.96	-0.07	0	1,015
22.00	1.56	1.68	1.64	+0.02	0	1,951
23.00	1.30	1.40	1.37	+0.02	0	2,627
24.00	1.11	1.21	1.11	-0.05	0	807
25.00	0.92	1.04	1.01	+0.03	0	6,309
26.00	0.70	0.98	0.92	+0.04	0	535
27.00	0.76	0.88	0.76	-0.05	0	562

This options chain provides information for just the calls on the stock, and some options chains are adjustable, allowing you to see puts and calls side by side or one on top of another. You want to be careful that you're looking at the type of option—either call or put—that you want to reference.

The options chain provides a wealth of details on GameStop calls that expire November 15, 2024, though if you want to see the details for different option expirations you can simply click to the relevant weeks or months. Along the left-hand rail are the strike prices, which for GameStop are denominated in increments of $1 because it is a highly traded and popular stock. Typically, option strikes are priced at $2.50 apart—$20, $22.50, $25, $27.50, and so on—though popular stocks like GameStop may have denominations in $1 increments or even less.

The chain also lists the last price that the option traded at and when that trade occurred, so you can know how stale that last quote is. Sometimes the last trade for a given strike occurred months ago, so the last quote is not a good measure of the current price. In this case it's better to look at the bid and ask prices to get a sense of where the option might trade currently. The chain also provides the option's price change from the day before and that day's trading volume.

The options chain provides a helpful piece of information called open interest. Open interest measures how many contracts are currently open for a given strike price. Some strikes may have no open interest, such as deep-in-the-money or deep-out-of-the-money options, while others may have tens of thousands of contracts or more, especially for strikes that are near the stock price. An options contract is opened whenever a trader sells to open or writes the contract. A contract is closed when a counterparty makes an offsetting trade—say, repurchasing a call that you sold—or a trader exercises the contract.

The options chain also gives you information about which monthly expirations are available for trading in each stock. Options for the current month and the next month are always available for stocks that have options trading. However, the availability of options for subsequent months depends on the options cycle for the specific stock. In other words, options are not available for every future month on a stock. So, the options chain also informs you which future expirations are available for trade as of now. As options expire, the chain will be updated with new expirations geared to a specific schedule.

HOW THE OPTIONS CYCLE WORKS

You may wonder how the options cycle works. As mentioned before, no stocks—not even the most popular ones—have options available for all future months over the coming year or two. So, you won't be able to buy just any old expiration that you're looking for. Instead, you'll have to make do with the available expirations. Options for each stock are rolled out on an assigned cycle, according to the following schedule:

- **Cycle 1:** January, April, July, October
- **Cycle 2:** February, May, August, November
- **Cycle 3:** March, June, September, December

Each stock has at least four available expirations: the current month, the forward month, and the next two expirations in its cycle. Here's how it works.

Imagine that you want to trade an option that's on Cycle 1 and that it's currently late December, past the third weekend of the month, when monthly options expire. Regardless of the cycle, a stock will always have the current month and the forward month (January and February in this case, respectively) available for trading. Then the option will also have the next two subsequent months in its cycle available. For example, up until the January expiration for a Cycle 1 option, the expiration would include January, February, April, and July. After the January option expires, the expirations would then be updated to include the next four expirations: February (the current month), March (the forward month), April, and July. After the February expiration, the new options would include March, April, July, and October—again, the next four expirations for Cycle 1.

While these are the standardly available options cycles, many high-volume stocks today also have a range of other expirations, including weekly expirations for the most popular stocks. In addition to these weekly options, high-volume stocks may also have long-term options that are called LEAPS, which stands for Long-Term Equity Anticipation Securities, that can expire up to three years in the future.

What's in a Name?

Despite the different names, the long-term options called LEAPS function just the same as the shorter-term versions. LEAPS give your investment thesis more time to work out, though they're available on only the most popular stocks and funds.

PLACING YOUR OPTIONS TRADE

Getting Your Trade Filled Correctly

You have your investment thesis and your options strategy, so it's now time to place your trade. Unlike stock trading, where you have only two choices for a given equity—buy or sell—with options, you have several different choices, any one of which you can get wrong. You can buy a call when you meant to buy a put, select the wrong strike price, or choose the wrong expiration, for example. So, it's time to run through the key aspects of placing an option trade so that you minimize your chances of error.

KEY ELEMENTS OF PLACING AN OPTION TRADE

When you place an option trade, you must input some variables before you can place the trade. You should know exactly what you want to trade before you even approach your broker's order-entry page, or you're apt to enter the wrong order.

- **Single-leg or multi-leg strategy:** Some trading platforms allow you to enter multi-leg strategies as a single order, though you can always enter them as separate single-leg orders, albeit with the caveats explained in the section on common pitfalls. The broker may have you specify the strategy, such as Buy-Write, where you buy the underlying stock and then sell a call.

- **Buy or sell:** You'll need to enter whether you're buying or selling the option.
- **Call or put:** You'll need to specify whether you're trading a call or put option for any single-leg orders.
- **Strike price:** Many options chains offer a huge range of strike prices. Commonly strike prices are in increments of $2.50, so a stock might have strikes $32.50, $35, $37.50, and so on. But high-volume stocks may offer increments of just $1. So, you could have a stock that has literally eleven different strike prices from $100 to $110 at every dollar mark.
- **Expiration:** Low-volume stocks will typically have just four expirations, according to its options cycle. High-volume stocks may have a much larger range of expirations, including those that extend out more than two years. You could easily have more than a dozen choices here.
- **Contracts:** You'll need to enter the number of contracts that you want to purchase or sell. Again, contracts are quoted in per-share figures ($1.75, $2.25, etc.), but the dollar value of that transaction is 100 times that figure (so $175, $225, and so on).
- **Market or limit order:** You can specify whether you want the trade to execute with a market order or a limit order. Choose a limit order, which allows you to name the price you want the trade to execute at. A market order leaves you at the mercy of traders.

When you're specifying a price for your limit order, one common strategy is to split the bid-ask spread, the difference between the buyer's bid price and the seller's asking price. For example, if the spread is $0.10, then name a price that's right in between the two—five cents higher than the bid and five cents lower than the ask. Don't be surprised if you don't get an immediate fill on the order, but be prepared to wait to see if the trade eventually fills. You can always adjust your price if the order is sitting out there a while. For wider bid-ask spreads, it can be advantageous to be more aggressive on pricing and then adjust your price as you discover that an order won't fill. You may get a better price than you expected. If you know a specific contract has filled at your price that day, it can be worthwhile to wait for it, especially if the stock is moving in a direction that makes the price possible.

Review your trade carefully, because you have a lot of different order details that need to be right. When you're confident the order is correct, hit the submit button.

COMMON ORDER-ENTRY PITFALLS

It can be easy to make a mistake when placing an order, and here are some common mistakes.

Entering the Wrong Trade

It's all too easy to input the wrong trade with options. One of the easiest mistakes is simply buying an option when you meant to sell it. And what's particularly dangerous with options is not just that you made the wrong trade, but that often you made exactly the opposite trade of what you intended. For example, you may want to buy a call, but you end up selling a call. Well, in that situation you just exposed your portfolio to unlimited loss. Worse, you're making the trade precisely because you expect the call to go up, or in other words for the short call to lose a lot of money. So, you've ended up doing exactly the trade that you wanted to avoid. Plus, it's even easier to make this error if you're trying to make an options trade quickly and take advantage of good pricing. The only solution is to realize your error and quickly reverse the trade, often at some expense. Of course, you should proofread your trades before you make them to avoid this error before it happens.

Entering a Multi-Leg Trade As Individual Orders

If you're entering multi-leg trades, it's advisable to enter each leg as part of a single trade with your broker. If you enter a multi-leg trade as separate orders, there's a possibility that you fill only one of the legs, leaving you unhedged and in a potentially risky position. Executing a multi-leg trade as a single unit prevents this. For multi-leg trades, you can set the pricing as a single number rather than specifying the prices of single legs separately. Of course, part of the beauty of options is that they allow you to do so many things, including setting up multi-leg trades well after you set up the first leg, but sometimes your order should go in all at once.

Pay or Get Paid

For a multi-leg trade, understand what a good price for each of the legs is and then determine the net price of the trade. The broker will charge you a net debit—the net cost of the legs—or offer you a net credit—the net premium you receive.

Using a Market Order

While you can use market orders for options trading, stick with limit orders, which allow you to name the price that you want the trade to execute at. Limit orders allow your trade to fill at a price that you expect and don't expose you to highly sensitive options prices.

LEGGING INTO OPTIONS TRADES

How to Open a Trade Smartly

Part of the beauty of options is that they are endlessly flexible. You can buy and sell pieces of a stock's risk profile at any point in time and for any available duration. If you own a stock and you don't think that it can go any higher in the next few months, sell a call option for every 100 shares you own and collect the premium. If the stock doesn't go over that price level at expiration, you keep the stock and the premium. (This strategy is called a covered call, and it's discussed later in the book.) Although stocks are more limited, you can combine options, ride them higher or lower, and then sell off a piece of the risk above or below a certain level. While traders may typically set up multi-leg strategies as a single trade at the same time, nothing says you must. Options give you the possibility to change your decision on the fly in response to market action, and you can "leg into" a multi-leg position at different moments in time. Here is how you can leg into an options strategy and what to watch out for.

ENTERING MULTI-LEG ORDERS AS A SINGLE ORDER

Legging into an options position is executing the legs of a multi-leg options strategy at different points. It can sometimes be an effective way to trade options, though it's often not prudent. You are well-advised to enter a multi-leg trade as a single order. A good brokerage allows you to enter the legs of the trade as one order with one net debit or one net credit rather than specifying prices for each leg. Not only is order entry easier this way, but it protects you from risk if you're unable to get your order filled on each separate leg. If you conceive of the multi-leg strategy as a single trade, enter it as a single trade and avoid a potentially nasty outcome if the pricing gets away from you.

Entering the legs as separate orders can lead to real heartache. Imagine a two-part trade using a lower-strike long call and a higher-strike short call, which is a bull call spread. Imagine if the order for the short call were filled before that of the long call. You suddenly have the unhedged risk of the short call without the protection of the long call. If the stock suddenly moves in an unfavorable direction (up in this case), you may not be able to get the order on the long call filled at an acceptable price. At the same time, the value of the short call rises, hurting your profit without the offsetting protection of the lower-priced long call. So, you're immediately on the losing end of a trade. At this point you have a few choices, none of which is great: (1) Purchase the long call at the new higher price, hurting the return on your spread trade; (2) Let the short call ride unhedged, perhaps with the hope that the stock price comes back down and you can buy the long call, potentially exposing you to significant loss if the stock keeps rising; or (3) Close the short call for an immediate loss.

For this reason, you're advised to enter multi-leg orders as single orders, ensuring that you get a fill on the various legs at the same time and protecting yourself in the process.

LEG INTO A TRADE ON THE FLY

The flexibility of options means that what started as one type of trade can quickly become another type if you spot an opportunity to profit. Take for instance the same example of a bull call spread to see how it might make sense to put on the two legs of the trade at different times.

Stock XYZ is priced at $50 per share and does not pay a dividend. After doing some research, you think this stock could be worth $70 and perhaps more in a year. Because of the large difference between the potential value and the current value, you decide to take an aggressive position using only a long call. A $57.50 call is available for $3.10 and expires in a year, and you buy one contract for $310. You decide on a long call on this trade because of the high potential upside and the potential that the stock could rise even higher if it gains momentum.

Six months later the stock has risen to $65 per share, and your call is now trading for $10. Great job! With six months remaining on the contract and the stock near your estimate of fair value, you're considering how to pivot on this trade. With its strong performance, the stock may even reach $75 in the contract's remaining time, but you don't think the stock is likely to go down much. You have a few potential choices at this juncture: (1) You could sell the call for $10 and pocket your profit of $690. (2) You could continue to hold on to the contract, because you expect further upside but recognize that the good run may not continue. With $2.50 in time value left on the contract, if the stock went nowhere for the rest of the period, your option would lose significant value. If the stock fell from $65 to $62.50 at expiration, your option would fall from $10 to $5, wiping out half your value. (3) You could sell a higher-priced call and leg into a bull call spread. Here you sell the stock's upside above some strike price and collect a premium for doing so. A $70 call is priced at $3.15; a $72.50 call is priced at $2.40; and a $75 call is priced at $1.80. If you sell one of those calls, you'll enjoy your long option's gains up to that level.

Don't Get Cute with Legging

Don't fall into the trap of thinking that legging into a trade later is super sophisticated. It's a trading decision to try to maximize profit. You started with one thesis, and then as events played out, you decided to pivot, using the flexibility of options.

If you choose to sell one of these calls, you're legging into a bull call spread, realizing a gain on the sold option, and you still have potential upside if the stock moves up. Selling the higher-priced call helps reduce your overall risk and allows you to "take money off the table." By legging into the trade, you can transform a long call strategy into a bull call spread later.

WHEN AND HOW TO EXIT YOUR OPTIONS TRADE

Closing Your Trade Intelligently

Knowing when to close out a trade is one of the hardest skills in investing, and even advanced investors and traders have difficulty closing a trade for maximum profit. This difficulty is compounded with options, which can move much more quickly than stocks and rapidly erase a profit. So, you need to actively manage your positions and be more aggressive when pricing becomes favorable. An attractive price—or maybe just the best price you'll be able to get—may be available only for a short time, and with time working constantly to erode the value of options, you must carefully consider the trade-off between risk and reward. But you have rules of thumb for how to close out an options trade.

HOW TO CLOSE OUT A TRADE

If you're trying to close a trade, in effect you take the opposite action of what you did to start the trade. If you "buy to open" the trade—going long a call or put—you'll "sell to close" to end the trade. Similarly, if you "sell to open" the trade—going short a call or put—you'll "buy to close" to end the trade. In other words, those with long options will need to sell to close their position, while those with short strategies will need to buy to close. Of course, the trade will automatically be closed once the option reaches expiration, but that may not offer a favorable outcome to you.

TIME VALUE AND WHEN
TO CLOSE A TRADE

Time value is particularly important when thinking about exiting an option trade. When the time value of an option is high, it makes no financial sense for you to exercise an option, since you would receive more value by simply selling the option. But as an option approaches expiration, particularly in the last couple months, its time value rapidly decays. As time value approaches zero, you as the option owner have less and less incentive not to exercise the contract if it otherwise makes sense, and you must assess whether you have any real chance at remaining upside by continuing to hold the option. Time keeps ticking, and the last weeks of a contract can become expensive.

Time decay is always working against an option owner, so you want to make sure you have potential upside if you continue to hold a position. You're on the hot seat and may need to act aggressively as the option enters its last two weeks. If you can sell when a stock moves favorably, you may want to jump on the chance. It's the same principle if you're trying to minimize a loss, selling if you get a favorable short-term move. Holding on and seeing the stock stagnate or move in an unfavorable direction virtually guarantees the option price moves lower. On the flip side, if you find yourself with a near-the-money option with little time value, you may decide to go for broke and hold close to expiration on the chance that the option makes a significant move and puts the option in the money, at the cost of losing any remaining premium.

It's a bit of a different calculation if you have an open short option, since time decay is working in your favor. You'll want to balance the chances of the option being exercised with how much you'll collect if you do hold through expiration. Options that are way out of the money may be worth holding to expiration, but close-to-the-money options with little time value may require a more careful calculation. You'll need to balance the reward of collecting the remaining premium on the option against the risk of the option going in the money in the final days of the contract.

For example, imagine you have a short put just out of the money, which is priced at $0.25 and is set to expire in a week. If you hold out, you may be able to collect that last morsel of premium, if the stock can stay out of the money (above the strike here) through expiration. For this potential gain, you risk a last-minute move in the stock that could push it in the money and cost you serious cash. Because of the negative risk-reward, many traders decide to settle for most of the profit rather than remain exposed to the last-minute risk. They close the short position by buying back the option, settling for perhaps 80% of the max premium rather than trying to earn 100% of it but endure the risk of a last-minute move.

EVALUATING RISK-REWARD ON A TRADE

If you're taking a fundamentals-based approach to trading options, which this book advocates, your research and investment thesis can help you make the decision to sell. If the stock has reached your estimate of its value and you see limited future gain, that could be the moment to close the position or partially close the position to remove some risk. If the stock has yet to reach that level, you'll need to consider whether it makes sense to continue holding based on how much time value remains. It may be better to close this trade, reevaluate your thesis, and then set up a similar trade again with a longer expiration, if you continue to believe in your thesis.

MECHANICAL SELLING

Traders may take a mechanical approach to closing out a profitable trade. For example, you may decide to close part of the trade once it's reached a certain profit level and then sell more when the remaining position increases by a further amount. Some traders look to take their original capital off the table once the trade has reached a certain level of profitability, taking a defensive posture so that they can maintain their trading capital. If you lose what's still at risk, at least you have the original money and can trade again.

If you are short options, it may make sense to close the trade once a certain portion of the premium has been collected, since short positions require substantial margin capacity.

CLOSING OUT MULTI-LEG STRATEGIES

If you're using multi-leg strategies, it's advisable to close out the strategy as a single trade, leaving yourself with no exposed risk—just as it's advisable to enter these trades as a single trade.

"Net" Out Your Trades

Closing out a multi-leg trade in one trade relieves you of the small or large chance that an event happens in the final days, sending an unhedged option soaring or plummeting. If the wrong move occurred and you had the wrong unhedged risk, you could lose significant money.

BUILDING AN INVESTMENT PORTFOLIO WITH OPTIONS

Key Ways to Manage Your Options Portfolio

Given the leverage and volatility of options, it's important that you manage the risks of options effectively. One strategy explained in the next chapter is to adjust the strike prices on the options you're using to mitigate their risk. But once you've made the trade, you can't do much to change the volatility and risk of that individual option. However, you can do several things at the portfolio level to help mitigate the effect of options on your overall investment portfolio. Of course, you could specialize in certain strategies, disregarding the risk of a market melt-up or meltdown, but it may cost you.

KEEP OPTIONS EXPOSURE TO A MODEST SIZE

If you're looking to start trading options, it's advisable to keep your options exposure to a relatively small portion of your total portfolio, perhaps 5%–10% of your total holdings. While your options amp up the potential risk and return, the much larger portion of your portfolio—typically stocks and investment funds—can act as ballast, helping to steady the portfolio's overall value.

When you're thinking about your allocation to options, it's particularly important to understand what your actual exposure is. Suppose you have a $100,000 portfolio and you devote $5,000 to options positions. On long options, the most you can lose is what you put into the trade. If you pay $500 for an option, your loss is capped at that amount. In this case, it amounts to 10% of your options exposure of $5,000. But the situation is different for short options, where your exposure can be much larger. If you sell a put with a strike price of $40 and the stock falls by 50% at expiration, you suddenly must come up with $4,000 to buy a stock that is immediately worth only $2,000 in the market. A whopping 40% of your options portfolio is blown out of the water.

Figure Your Worst-Case Exposure

If you have several short put positions open at the same time and the market drops, your options exposure quickly becomes much greater than the target allocation you had planned on. Carefully calculate your options exposure so that you're not running too much risk.

KEEP YOUR PORTFOLIO TO JUST A FEW OPTIONS

If you're looking to just do a little bit of options trading, perhaps layering on an options trade to a stock you already own or are watching, you could do so without specifying a percentage of your portfolio. You could have a well-diversified portfolio of stocks and funds and then just add on a contract or two that you think looks attractively priced. You'll still want to make sure the exposure isn't too high, but options can be simply a sideline to your normal investments.

SPECIALIZE IN ONE TYPE OF OPTIONS STRATEGY

If you'd like to specialize in one type of options strategy—perhaps you like long calls—no one's stopping you from taking that approach. But it does present certain risks as outlined previously, so you'll want to mitigate those risks in other ways, such as using different expirations. Active management may also help mitigate risk, as you realize profits on positions with an unfavorable risk-reward ratio.

DIVERSIFY YOUR OPTIONS PORTFOLIO

Whether you're devoting your entire portfolio to options or just a portion of your portfolio, it can make sense to use a variety of different strategies to help reduce risk. The high sensitivity of option prices to stock prices means that even small changes in the underlying asset can drastically alter the value of options, and particularly so for options near the money. You want to avoid a massive drop occurring and sinking your options portfolio, and given the nature of options, you could diversify by underlying asset, by expiration date, and by strategy. A portfolio that offers some balance can give you needed capital when the market works against you and just when you need it.

By Underlying Asset
You can reduce your concentration in options that are on the same underlying stock or other underlying stocks that have a high

correlation. For example, you want to avoid making all your option bets on the same stock, because if something happens to that stock, you may hold a bunch of worthless contracts or have the stock put to you at a significant loss. Similarly, you may want to avoid stocks that have high correlations with one another. For example, stocks in the same industry are affected by the same fundamental factors, so they may move in sync, meaning you get less diversification if you own options on a few of them. In contrast, you could purchase options on stocks in different industries that may not have a lot of correlation.

By Time

The stock market can fall or rise at any time and for reasons that have nothing to do with the stock you have options on. Maybe the market "corrects" by falling 10% or more from a high. If you own an option that expires soon and a major dislocation hits the market just then, it could turn a major profit into a loss. If you have a full options portfolio, this move could hit you hard, but it's going to be even worse if a huge portion of your options expire soon. So, one of the strategies to mitigate this impact is to diversify your options' expirations. You could own contracts that expire over a few months, then six to eight months, and then perhaps a year or longer.

Short-term events such as a correction are one reason that options traders need to actively manage their portfolio. If you've eked out most of the gain on a contract, there may be little sense in sticking around to get the last bit of it if a short-term event could cause your profit to plummet.

By Options Strategy

Another way to protect an options portfolio against short-term events is to use a variety of strategies that may respond differently in different environments. For example, if you own a long call, which may do well when the market is rising, it could make sense to balance that with a strategy that gets a little extra tailwind in a falling market, such as a long put.

MORE SOPHISTICATED STRATEGIES

Advanced options traders may hone additional strategies to mitigate the risks on their portfolio, and one of the most prevalent is what is known as delta hedging, after the option Greek of delta. With this strategy, you use stock to hedge your options position based on the option's sensitivity to the stock (its delta). It typically requires a regular adjustment of the hedge as the option's delta changes, making it a more intensive approach to risk mitigation.

HOW OPTIONS TRADERS FAIL

Common Ways to Fail and How to Avoid Them

Legendary investor Charlie Munger used to advise investors to avoid failure if they want to succeed. That is, he told people to determine what would make them fail a task and then to be sure to avoid doing those things. In that spirit, here are some of the most common ways that traders fail when they trade options.

UNDERESTIMATING HOW LONG IT WILL TAKE THE MARKET TO MOVE

The job of an options trader is much harder than that of a stock trader. You not only have to do the fundamental research on a stock to know which way it's likely to move in the future, but you also must set up the options trade that can capture this movement. So, your investment thesis must be right, and you must time it correctly. If you're buying options, time is not your friend. Every day the value of your long options is declining, hurting your profits. You're on the clock, and the closer you are to expiration, the more rapidly that time value will decay. Your investment thesis can ultimately be 100% right, but if the stock doesn't move before expiration, your trade is still a loser. Because of this double constraint on the options trade, it's important that you give your trade enough time to work out. The more time you give your option trade to work, the greater the possibility that a correct investment thesis will bear out.

It Always Takes Longer Than You Think

While a stock may seem obviously undervalued to you, it can take the market a long time to come around to your vision of value. That's not even factoring in the market's inevitable hiccups along the way, which can disrupt your option trade in the short term.

OVERLOOKING THE ADVANTAGES OF SELLING OPTIONS

You don't have to look too hard to see the advantages of going long on options—namely, the potential to multiply your money many times. However, while these "home runs" are nice, they can be difficult to come by, and so some traders choose to also sell options and generate smaller, more consistent wins. Short strategies have the advantage of putting the wind at your back, allowing time decay to work in your favor rather than against you. Similarly, you can also take advantage in periods of high volatility, selling options when they're relatively expensive and then letting time and declining volatility slowly reduce the options' value. So, if options look relatively expensive, maybe it's time to sell them instead of being a buyer. You can use the Greeks to help you find what's attractively priced, and many brokers offer options tools that can help you find good opportunities.

TRYING TO GET EVERY LAST CENT OF PROFIT

With short options strategies, it can be tempting to wait and let the option expire so you can collect the last few cents of the premium. But it may not make sense if you're likely to get only a little bit of profit and have some chance that you may lose more money. It can be what some wits call "picking up nickels in front of steamrollers," the definition of a poor risk-reward ratio. You may get run over if the stock moves against you, all for a pittance.

NOT ACTIVELY MANAGING YOUR OPTIONS

With stocks, you have the luxury of time to wait out a market downturn, but options give you no such benefit. You need to carefully watch your options, understand how they're performing compared to your goals, actively set up new trades, and prune old ones. A well-diversified portfolio of options may have trades expiring every week or at least every month, and you won't be able to step away for weeks at a time, as you could for a stock portfolio. You'll need to decide whether it makes sense to close out short trades where you've earned most of the premium already, and you'll also need to realize when holding on to the risk for a short period no longer makes sense. You must determine whether it makes sense to close out winning trades and when. To actively manage your options portfolio, you want a trading plan that helps you make decisions.

FAILING TO HAVE A TRADING PLAN

If you don't have a trading plan, you're flying blind with options trading. A trading plan offers well-thought-out rules that can guide your trading, so you don't always need to actively consider what the best course of action is and how you're going to manage your portfolio. Your trading plan can help you decide how to put on trades and manage your portfolio, and it can give you the overall picture of how you'll approach trading. It can help you decide which risks to take and when to trim those risks. A good trading plan also outlines the strategies you'll use, the information needed to justify a trade, and position sizing. A good trading plan answers key questions that you'll encounter regularly and provides you with guidance on them so that you can stick to an approach that works and avoid veering into a morass of mistakes.

NOT FACTORING IN BID-ASK SPREADS AND NOT USING LIMIT ORDERS

You may have found an interesting trade, but what's the bid-ask spread on it? Illiquid options can quickly eat up your capital with their spreads, especially when you're making an opening or closing trade. So, it's vital that you factor in bid-ask spreads to your cost of trading or otherwise stick to more liquid options. Be sure to use limit orders when you place trades, and don't be afraid to put in a low bid and then inch it up to see if you can get a better price.

SIZING YOUR POSITION INCORRECTLY

If you're used to the world of stock trading, it can be easy to forget how much leverage options can give you and how quickly they can move in one direction or another. It's all to say that you need to be careful about sizing your options positions correctly. While a 10% down move in the stock might hurt, the same move might wipe out your options position entirely. You can't afford a 100% loss on a substantial portion of your bankroll. That "sure thing" options trade may perform great for a while, but if you're overallocated to it and it doesn't work out, your portfolio could be sunk permanently. A good trading plan can help you size your positions correctly and maintain your discipline.

Chapter 4

Basic Options Strategies

This chapter presents the four core options strategies that allow you to wager on the upward and downward movements of stocks and other assets. These four strategies are based on the two fundamental options—the call and the put—and they form the "bread and butter" of any trader's tool kit. It's vital to understand these strategies thoroughly because they can come in handy in many different situations. As discussed earlier, these "single-leg" strategies form the basis of all other advanced strategies, so being fluent in these core elements is essential to success.

Understanding these core strategies is also important because you may build advanced strategies as you go along—as part of "shift-on-the-fly" trading—rather than as discrete "multi-leg" strategies that you always build from scratch. In other words, you may decide to purchase a call option at one point in time and then later decide that selling a call at a higher strike price is an attractive strategy. Voilà—you created an advanced strategy by putting together two basic strategies at distinct points in time. For reasons such as this it's vital to know the benefits, drawbacks, and right situations for these core strategies.

LONG CALL

Multiply Your Money with the Long Call

A good place to start discussing the four core options strategies is with the long call. This is the kind of option people think of when they think of making big money in the options market, and it can certainly have this result, if used properly.

With a long call you purchase a call, and the call has the potential to appreciate many times in value until its expiration. The potential downside is capped at the premium paid for the call.

WHEN TO USE THE LONG CALL

By itself, the long call is a good strategy when the underlying stock has a long runway to rise. That long runway could be due to any number of factors: the company's strong growth prospects, strong momentum, increasing earnings, a hot new product, and so on. The point is: The long call is a good setup for a stock that can continue to rise for the length of the option's lifetime.

HOW TO MODIFY THE LONG CALL TO CALIBRATE RISK AND RETURN

You can modify the long call to help adjust your risk and return, allowing you to take less risk and earn a lower potential return, or turn the dial up on risk and increase the potential return—if you're right. For example, you could make the following adjustments: **(1) Base case:** Purchase a just-out-of-the-money call option; **(2) More risk, more return:** Purchase an out-of-the-money call option, say, at a strike that is $5 or $7.50 higher than the current stock price; or **(3) Less risk, less return:** Purchase an in-the-money call option, say, at a strike that is $2.50 or $5 lower than the current stock price.

Balancing Risk and Reward

Lowering the call's strike increases the odds that the stock will be above the strike at expiration, and you exchange a lower risk of total loss for a lower total return. With a higher strike, you opt for higher potential return with increased odds of losing the entire premium.

THE PROFIT POTENTIAL OF A LONG CALL

Consider the example of Stock ABC trading for $40 per share. In the base case, you can buy a call option with a strike price of $42.50 with an expiration in six months for $2.50. Here is the profit on the trade with the stock price at expiration, including two other scenarios.

Three variations of the long call

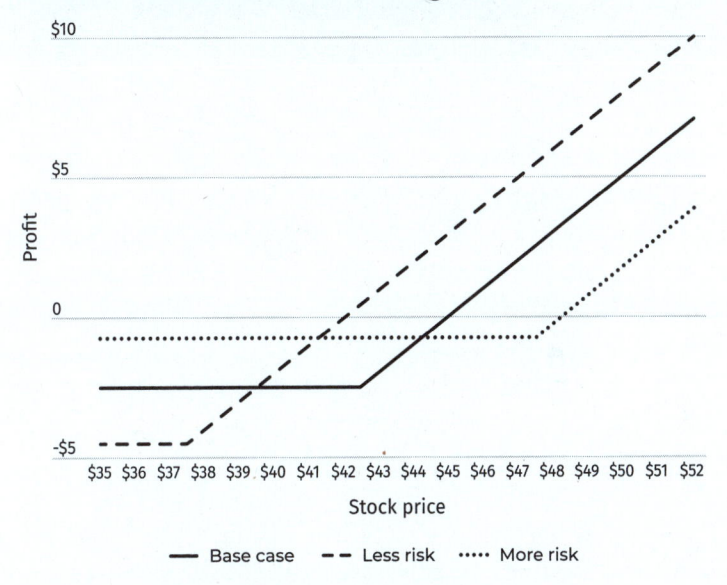

First look at the numbers on the base case:

- At the strike price of $42.50, the option goes in the money. However, at this price at expiration, the option expires worthless, and you lose the full premium of $2.50.
- At any stock price below the $42.50 strike, the option expires worthless, and you lose the full premium of $2.50.
- Above the strike price, every $1 rise in the stock price at expiration increases the option's price by $1. This trade does not break even until the stock price hits $45, or the $42.50 strike plus the $2.50 premium.

But the other lines on the graph ratchet up and down the risk to see how you could match your expectations of the stock's performance with different strikes.

Lower-Risk Example

In the lower-risk example, Stock ABC is still at $40 per share, and you can buy a call option with a strike price of $37.50 with an expiration in six months for $4.50. Here are the risks and payoffs for this lower-risk long call:

- At the strike price of $37.50, the option goes in the money. However, at this price or below at expiration, the option expires worthless, with you losing the premium of $4.50.
- Above the strike price, every $1 rise in the stock price at expiration increases the option's price by $1. In this trade, you don't break even until the stock price hits $42, or the $37.50 strike plus the $4.50 premium.

Higher-Risk Example

In the final example, the risk moves up. Stock ABC is still at $40, and you can buy a call option with a strike price of $47.50 with an expiration in six months for $0.75. Here are the risks and payoffs for this higher-risk long call:

- At the strike price of $47.50, the option goes in the money. However, at this price or below at expiration, the option expires worthless, with you losing the full premium of $0.75.
- Above the strike price, every $1 rise in the stock price at expiration increases the option's price by $1. This trade does not break even until the stock price hits $48.25, or the $47.50 strike plus the $0.75 premium.

KEY TAKEAWAYS

Use the provided table to compare these scenarios to see how they stack up in terms of gains and losses, assuming a range of outcomes for the stock.

Stock price at expiration	Stock price change (from $40)	Profit on low risk (strike at $37.50, cost of $4.50)	Profit on medium risk (strike at $42.50, cost of $2.50)	Profit on high risk (strike at $47.50, cost of $0.75)
$35	−12.5%	−$4.50	−$2.50	−$0.75
$37.50	−6.25%	−$4.50	−$2.50	−$0.75
$40	0%	−$2.00	−$2.50	−$0.75
$42.50	6.25%	$0.50	−$2.50	−$0.75
$45	12.5%	$3.00	$0	−$0.75
$47.50	18.75%	$5.50	$2.50	−$0.75
$50	25%	$8.00	$5.00	$1.75
$52.50	31.25%	$10.50	$7.50	$4.25
Max loss		−$4.50	−$2.50	−$0.75
Max gain (%, up to $52.50)		133%	200%	467%

The takeaway here for you is that a lower-risk strategy exchanges the lower risk of a total loss of premium for a lower percentage upside (133%), though you have to put more premium on the table. If the stock dips from $40, the lower-risk trade has a chance of keeping some premium, while the other strategies will not keep any.

The higher-risk trade requires the stock to move up substantially to avoid losing it all, from $40 to above the $47.50 strike. If the stock stayed where it was when the trade was put on, you would lose the whole premium, though it is smaller. If the stock rises significantly, this trade has the highest-potential upside at $52.50 (and above), earning a huge 467%. Here you exchange a high probability of loss for a much higher percentage gain, if you're correct. The middle case falls in the middle, of course.

You'll need to understand these trade-offs between risk and return to successfully put on your trades, and you'll need to calibrate them to your expectations of the stock's performance.

SHORT CALL

With a short call, you sell or "write" a call, and the premium received from the buyer is the maximum total return. The potential downside is theoretically unlimited, in a case where the stock continues to soar until expiration. If you sell a call by itself, it's termed an uncovered call. In contrast, if you sell a call against your stake in the underlying stock, it's a less risky strategy named a covered call, which will be discussed in Chapter 5. If this segment looks familiar as you're reading, it should, since all the expected payoffs and losses are simply the reverse of those for the long call.

WHEN TO USE THE SHORT CALL

The short call can be used when the underlying stock is expected to stay or go below the strike price by expiration. You want to be sure that the stock is unlikely to rise significantly before the option's expiration, because it could create substantial losses.

Short Calls Are Not Free

While a short call may seem like free money, you are bearing the risk of the stock rising significantly until the option expires, a situation that could lead to a massive loss.

HOW TO MODIFY THE SHORT CALL TO CALIBRATE RISK AND RETURN

You can adjust the strike price on the short call to modify your risk and return, taking less risk and earning a lower return or trying to earn a greater return with more risk. For example, you could recalibrate as follows: **(1) Base case:** Sell a just out-of-the-money call, **(2) More risk, more return:** Sell an in-the-money call at a strike that is $2.50 or $5 lower than the stock price, or **(3) Less risk, less return:** Sell an out-of-the-money call at a strike that is $5 or $7.50 higher than the stock price.

For the short call, raising the strike price decreases the odds the stock price will be above the strike at expiration. You exchange a lower risk of losing any money for a lower total return. Meanwhile, a lower strike increases the premium but also increases the odds of not receiving the entire premium, since the option is already in the money.

An Interesting Inverse Relationship

The risk-reward for the short call is the reverse of that for the long call. What is riskier for the long call is less risky for the short call, and vice versa. Remember, options are really just a zero-sum game between traders.

THE PROFIT POTENTIAL OF A SHORT CALL

The maximum profit potential of a short call is limited to the premium received for selling the option. The downside of a short call is uncapped and depends on how the stock performs.

Returning to the example, assume again that Stock ABC is trading at $40. In the base case, you can sell a $42.50 call with an expiration in six months for $2.50. This graph shows the profit on the base case as well as on the higher-risk and lower-risk trades.

Three variations of the short call

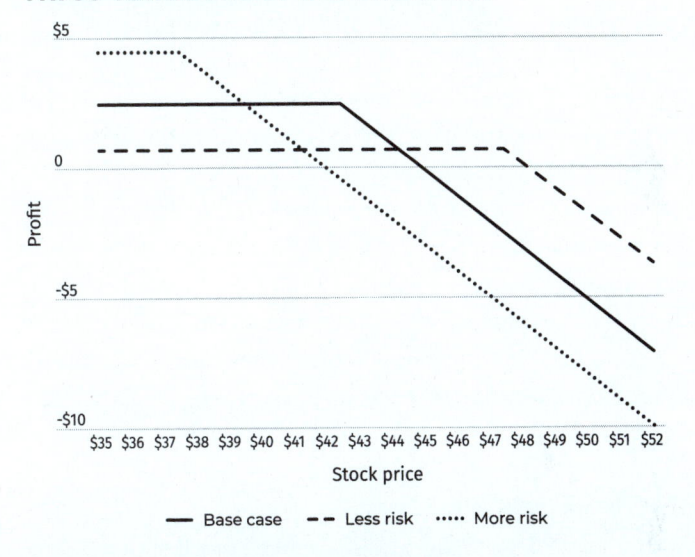

Look at the numbers on the base case:

- At the $42.50 strike, the option goes in the money. At this price and below at expiration, the option expires worthless, with you keeping the full premium of $2.50.
- At stock prices between $42.50 and $45, you keep part of the premium but not all of it. Every $1 increase in the stock reduces your profit by $1.
- Above $45 at expiration (the strike plus the $2.50 premium), you lose more money than was received with the premium. Every $1 rise in the stock price at expiration reduces your profit by $1. The short call will lose money overall as the stock continues to rise.

Lower-Risk Example

You can adjust the risk up and down to see how you could use the strike prices to match your expectations of the stock's performance. First, try reducing the risk. Stock ABC trades at $40 and this example will have you sell a $47.50 call with an expiration in six months at $0.75. Here are the risks and payoffs for this lower-risk short call:

- At the $47.50 strike, the option goes out of the money. At this price or below at expiration, the option expires worthless, with you keeping the full premium.
- Between $47.50 and $48.25 at expiration, you earn some but not all the premium. Every increase in the stock decreases your profit by a similar amount.
- If the stock rises above $48.25 at expiration (the strike plus the $0.75 premium), you would lose more money than received with the premium. Every $1 rise in the stock decreases the profit by $1. This lower-risk short call has no cap on the loss.

Higher-Risk Example

Consider again Stock ABC at $40 and sell a call with a $37.50 strike with an expiration in six months for $4.50. Here are the risks and rewards for this higher-risk short call:

- At the $37.50 strike, the option goes out of the money. At this price or below at expiration, the call expires worthless, and you keep the full premium of $4.50.
- Between the stock prices of $37.50 and $42 at expiration, you earn some of the premium. Every $1 rise in the stock decreases the profit by $1.

- If the stock rises above $42 at expiration (the strike plus the $4.50 premium), you begin to lose money on a net basis. Each $1 increase reduces your profit by $1. This short call has no cap on the potential loss.

KEY TAKEAWAYS

Compare these scenarios to see how their gains and losses stack up.

Stock price at expiration	Stock price change (from $40)	Profit on high risk (strike at $37.50, cost of $4.50)	Profit on medium risk (strike at $42.50, cost of $2.50)	Profit on low risk (strike at $47.50, cost of $0.75)
$35	–12.5%	$4.50	$2.50	$0.75
$37.50	–6.25%	$4.50	$2.50	$0.75
$40	0%	$2.00	$2.50	$0.75
$42.50	6.25%	–$0.50	$2.50	$0.75
$45	12.5%	–$3.00	$0	$0.75
$47.50	18.75%	–$5.50	–$2.50	$0.75
$50	25%	–$8.00	–$5.00	–$1.75
$52.50	31.25%	–$10.50	–$7.50	–$4.25
Max loss ($, up to $52.50)		–$10.50	–$7.50	–$4.25
Max gain		$4.50	$2.50	$0.75

Look back at the table for the long call. All the profits and losses are simply reversed from here.

A lower-risk strategy exchanges a lower risk of total loss of premium—the chance that the stock will go over $48.25—for a lower premium of $0.75. In contrast, if the stock rises just 5% from $40, the high-risk trade begins to lose money beyond the premium received, and it loses more than the others at each higher stock price. The medium-risk trade keeps the whole premium at any stock price below $42.50 at expiration, and the lower-risk trade keeps the premium below $47.50, a less likely scenario.

It's important to understand the trade-offs between risk and return, especially with a short call, because of the huge loss if the stock rises significantly. You do not want to be the trader who is "picking up nickels in front of a steamroller."

LONG PUT

The long put has certain similarities with the long call and offers the similar possibility of multiplying your money many times. The key difference is that the long put profits when the underlying stock falls, unlike the long call, which rises alongside the underlying stock.

With a long put, you purchase a put, and a put has the potential to multiply in value until its expiration. The potential downside is limited to the premium paid for the put. The maximum value of the long put is the total value of the stock at the strike price. For example, an option with a strike price of $42 has a maximum value of $4,200, or $42 × 100 shares per contract, if the stock goes to $0.

WHEN TO USE THE LONG PUT

The long put is a good strategy to use when the underlying stock can fall substantially. The reason for that fall could be anything: a stock with a high valuation or slowing growth, poor market sentiment, falling earnings, failing products, or any other reason. The upshot is: The long put is a good setup for a stock that can fall and continue to fall for the length of the option's lifetime.

HOW TO MODIFY THE LONG PUT TO CALIBRATE RISK AND RETURN

You can modify the long put to adjust your risk and return to match your expectations for the underlying asset's performance. So, you can take less risk and lower potential return or pump up the risk and increase the potential return. As with other basic strategies, you can make the following adjustments: **(1) Base case:** Purchase a just out-of-the-money put option; **(2) More risk, more return:** Purchase an out-of-the-money put, perhaps at a strike that is $5 or $7.50 lower—or more, if you dare—than the current stock price; or **(3) Less risk, less return:** Purchase an in-the-money put option at a strike that is $2.50 or $5 higher than the current stock price.

Raising the Odds of Success

Raising the strike price on a put increases the odds that the stock will be below the strike at expiration, so you exchange a lower risk of total loss for a lower total return. A lower strike trades higher potential returns for higher odds of losing the entire premium.

THE PROFIT POTENTIAL OF A LONG PUT

Consider again the example of Stock ABC trading for $40 per share. Suppose that you suspect that Stock ABC's earnings are poised to fall over the coming year. In the base case, you'll buy a put with a strike price of $37.50 with an expiration in six months for $2.50. In the graph, you'll see the profit from this trade as well as the more risky and less risky trades.

Three variations of the long put

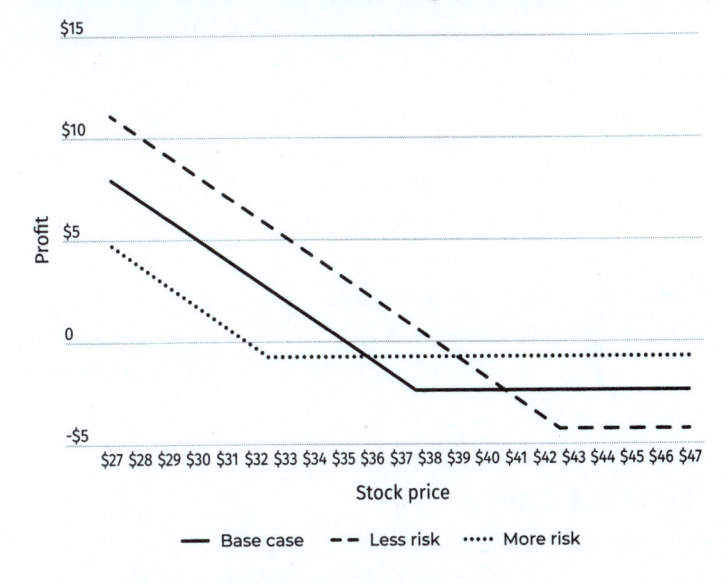

Look at the numbers on the base case:

- At the strike price of $37.50, the put goes in the money. However, if the stock sits at this price or anywhere above at expiration, the option would expire worthless, with you losing the full premium of $2.50.
- Below the strike price, every $1 fall in the stock at expiration increases the option's price by $1. This trade does not break even until the stock hits $35, or the $37.50 strike minus the $2.50 premium.

Lower-Risk Example

Now you'll calibrate the trade to see how to lower the risk and return. In this scenario, Stock ABC is still trading at $40 per share, and you'd like to buy a put with a strike of $42.50 with an expiration in six months for $4.50. Here's how it shakes out for this lower-risk long put:

- At the strike price of $42.50, the put goes in the money, meaning at the current $40, the stock is already in the money. However, at $42.50 or above at expiration, the option would expire worthless, with a loss of the full premium of $4.50.
- Below the strike price, every $1 fall in the stock price at expiration increases the option's price by $1. This trade does not break even until the stock falls below $38, or the $42.50 strike minus the $4.50 premium.

Higher-Risk Example

In the last example, increase the risk. Stock ABC is still at $40, and you'll buy a put with a strike price of $32.50 with an expiration in six months for $0.75. Here are the risks and payoffs for this higher-risk long put:

- The option goes in the money at $32.50, and at any price above this at expiration, the put expires worthless, with a loss of the whole premium of $0.75.
- Below the strike price, every $1 fall in the stock price at expiration increases the put's price by $1. Here the trade does not break even until $31.75, or the $32.50 strike minus the $0.75 premium.

KEY TAKEAWAYS

As before, compare these three scenarios in a table.

Stock price at expiration	Stock price change (from $40)	Profit on low risk (strike at $42.50, cost of $4.50)	Profit on medium risk (strike at $37.50, cost of $2.50)	Profit on high risk (strike at $32.50, cost of $0.75)
$27.50	–31.25%	$10.50	$7.50	$4.25
$30	–25%	$8.00	$5.00	$1.75
$32.50	–18.75%	$5.50	$2.50	–$0.75
$35	–12.5%	$3.00	$0	–$0.75
$37.50	–6.25%	$0.50	–$2.50	–$0.75
$40	0%	–$2.00	–$2.50	–$0.75
$42.50	6.25%	–$4.50	–$2.50	–$0.75
$45	12.5%	–$4.50	–$2.50	–$0.75
Max loss		–$4.50	–$2.50	–$0.75
Max gain (%, down to $27.50)		133%	200%	467%

As with the long call, the key takeaway for the long put is that a lower-risk strategy trades the reduced risk of a total loss of premium for a lower percentage upside (133%), and you must put more on the table in the form of the premium. Even if the stock rises somewhat above $40, the lower-risk trade has a chance of keeping some of that premium, while the riskier strategies are total losers.

In contrast, the higher-risk trade needs the stock to move down a lot to avoid becoming a total loss, from $40 to less than $32.50. In this scenario you exchange a high probability of loss for a higher percentage gain, if correct. If the stock simply stays at the $40 price when the trade was put on, you lose the entire premium, even if it's a smaller $0.75. If the stock falls significantly, this trade has the most percentage upside at $27.50 (or below), earning 467%.

The long put and its potential to multiply money many times may look like those of the long call. However, the profit on the long call is unlimited, while the long put's profit is limited to the total value of the strike price minus the premium. In either case, you need to calibrate your strikes to your expectations of the stock's performance.

SHORT PUT

Create Income by Selling Puts

Finally, this book has come to the short put, the last of the four basic options strategies. All the expected payoffs and losses are the reverse of those for the long put.

With a short put, you sell or write a put, and the premium received from the buyer is the total potential return from the trade. The potential downside is limited to the strike price of the put, if the stock or other underlying asset goes to $0. If the stock price is below the strike at expiration, you must buy the stock at the strike price.

The short put has certain similarities with the short call in that it offers a similar one-time premium payment. A key difference is that the short call has the potential for uncapped losses, while losses on the short put are limited, even if substantial.

WHEN TO USE THE SHORT PUT

The short put is a good strategy to use when the underlying stock is likely to stay flat or rise until the option's expiration. If the stock rises, the put is likely to expire worthless, meaning you keep the entire premium. You may think of this strategy as similar to insurance, with the put writer as the insurance company collecting the premium.

A short put can also be an attractive strategy if you would like to purchase the stock at a more favorable price. So, you could write a put with a strike at or below the current stock price, receive cash, and only have to pay for the stock if it falls below the strike. If the stock does not reach the strike by expiration, the put is unlikely to be exercised and you can repeat the trade, until the put is actually exercised, if ever.

HOW TO MODIFY THE SHORT PUT TO CALIBRATE RISK AND RETURN

You can modify the short put to adjust your risk and return to match your expectations of the underlying stock. You can lower or raise the risk and potential return: **(1) Base case:** Write a just out-of-the-money put; **(2) More risk, more return:** Write an in-the-money put, perhaps at a strike that is $2.50 or $5 higher than the current stock price; or **(3) Less risk, less return:** Write an out-of-the-money put, perhaps at a strike that is $5 or $7.50 lower than the current stock price.

A short put may expire worthless, but raising the strike price increases the odds that the stock will be below the strike at expiration, creating a greater likelihood that you will be put the stock.

Putting the Odds in Your Favor

By using a higher strike on a short put, you exchange a higher risk of being put the stock for a greater total premium. However, by selling a lower strike you opt for a lower total premium, with lower odds of having the option exercised.

THE PROFIT POTENTIAL OF A SHORT PUT

Back to the example of Stock ABC trading for $40. You expect Stock ABC to continue to rise over the period of the put, so you sell a $37.50 put with an expiration in six months for $2.50. Here's the profit on the base case at expiration at various stock prices as well as on the more risky and less risky scenarios.

Three variations of the short put

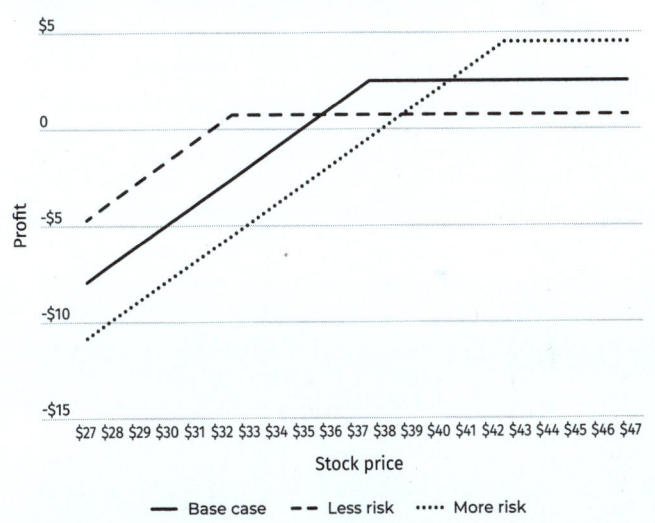

Look at the numbers on the base case:

- At the strike price of $37.50, the put goes in the money. However, if the stock sits at this price or above at expiration, the put expires worthless, earning the full premium of $2.50.

- Between the strike price and the breakeven price of $35 (the strike price minus the $2.50 premium), you earn some of the premium but not all of it.
- Below $35, every $1 fall in the stock at expiration increases your loss by $1.

Lower-Risk Example

Now lower the risk and return. Stock ABC is still trading for $40, and you'd like to sell a put with a strike price of $32.50 for $0.75. Here is the value of the short put at expiration and the profit:

- At the strike price of $32.50, the put goes in the money. At this price or above at expiration, the put expires worthless, earning the full premium of $0.75.
- Between $32.50 and the breakeven price of $31.75 (the strike price minus $0.75), you earn some of the premium but not all.
- Below the breakeven price, every $1 fall in the stock price at expiration increases the loss by $1.

Higher-Risk Example

For the final example, take the risk up and sell a put with a $42.50 strike price for $4.50. Here are the risks and payoffs for this higher-risk short put:

- The option goes in the money at the $42.50 strike, meaning that it's already in the money when it's written. If the stock reaches the strike price or more at expiration, the put expires worthless and you keep the whole premium.
- Between $42.50 and $38 (the strike minus the $4.50 premium), you earn part of the premium but not all. So, even if the stock

didn't move from $40 until expiration, you earn only a net $2 of the $4.50 premium.

- Below $38, every $1 decline in the stock price leads to a $1 decrease in profit.

KEY TAKEAWAYS

Compare these three scenarios in a table to see how it all works.

Stock price at expiration	Stock price change (from $40)	Profit on high risk (strike at $42.50, cost of $4.50)	Profit on medium risk (strike at $37.50, cost of $2.50)	Profit on low risk (strike at $32.50, cost of $0.75)
$27.50	−31.25%	−$10.50	−$7.50	−$4.25
$30	−25%	−$8.00	−$5.00	−$1.75
$32.50	−18.75%	−$5.50	−$2.50	$0.75
$35	−12.5%	−$3.00	$0	$0.75
$37.50	−6.25%	−$0.50	$2.50	$0.75
$40	0%	$2.00	$2.50	$0.75
$42.50	6.25%	$4.50	$2.50	$0.75
$45	12.5%	$4.50	$2.50	$0.75
Max gain		$4.50	$2.50	$0.75
Max loss ($, down to $27.50)		−$10.50	−$7.50	−$4.25

These dollar amounts are the opposite of those for the long put. With the short put the lower-risk strategy uses a lower strike price to reduce the chance of the option being exercised but offers a smaller premium. In contrast, the higher-risk put offers more premium but also a greater chance the option is exercised, since it is already in the money when written. The stock must rise by expiration for you to claim the entire premium.

The short put and the short call may look similar in terms of how they generate profit by receiving the premium. But it's important to note that the loss on the short put is limited to the total value of the "insured" stock, while the short call can expose you to unlimited loss.

DON'T OVERLOOK BASIC OPTIONS STRATEGIES

The Backbone of Options Trading

It can be easy to overlook these four options strategies as stand-alone strategies because they're basic. Beginners may look at these core strategies and scoff, because they're not the "sophisticated" advanced strategies. They may say that, while it's important to learn them, you need to move beyond these basics and use the advanced strategies "where the real money is made." However, these core strategies make up every options trade, regardless of how advanced it is. In fact, you need to be completely fluent in how these four strategies operate and how to calibrate them for those more advanced trades. When you're devising options strategies on the fly, you'll need to know the risks and rewards of picking a specific strategy and strike price, making these core strategies "must haves" in terms of comprehension.

WHEN THE CORE OPTIONS WORK BEST

You must comprehend the situations to which these four core strategies are best suited. The two long strategies—the long call and the long put—allow you to enjoy a stock's movement in one direction for the duration of the option. Pick the right trade, and you can multiply your money many times. The two short strategies—the short call and the short put—sell that potential risk and reward; these are better suited for traders looking to generate income repeatedly and take advantage of the decaying time value of these financial derivatives. In contrast, advanced strategies overlay two, three, and sometimes four or more other options to buy and sell bits and pieces of the stock's risk and reward, allowing you to break off and sell the less attractive aspects of the stock's performance profile for a price.

Remember: These core strategies give you lots of room to calibrate your trade so that it meets your expectations of a stock's performance. Yes, each strategy can be fine-tuned for risk and reward by choosing the appropriate strike prices, but options also allow you to adjust the time frame for your trade, giving you a completely other dimension. So, when talking about the four core strategies, it's important to realize that many high-volume stocks offer you literally hundreds of choices, between long and short, strike prices, and expiration dates. So, these four basic strategies are much more than just four choices when you belly up to the options chain. On the most popular stocks, you may have literally thousands of potential contracts to select from.

Know the Core Four

The four basic options strategies form the backbone of every options trade you'll make, even the advanced trades. Know these four strategies inside and out so that you'll be able to confidently set up trades and adjust existing trades as opportunities develop.

Not only are these four strategies the building blocks for everything else, but they're also some of the best strategies on their own. So, it's not a question of which strategy—the basics or more advanced multi-leg strategies—is better in some absolute sense; after all, you wouldn't use an advanced chain saw instead of a hammer to pound in a nail. It's a question of which options strategy is best for a given trading situation. Each strategy is a tool in your tool belt that you'll use when it's best for the job.

DON'T LET YOUR EGO DIRECT YOUR STRATEGY

Newer traders often let their egos direct their trading, and this approach can be tremendously detrimental to their success. Often, they want to make big trades and move around huge amounts of money, and options trading can certainly do both of those. For some, moving around large amounts of money is an ego trip. Others may see advanced options strategies in a similar light. They may decide that an advanced strategy is what they want, even if it doesn't match the trading setup that they've identified. For example, you might want to use a bull call spread (explained in Chapter 6) instead of a long call on a stock that has an extended runway for growth. In the right circumstances, any one of the various options strategies can be the right one, but a bull call spread may not be appropriate for a stock that has substantial upside. In contrast, a long call allows you to capture all the potential upside in a stock's bull run until the expiration of the option. You may have identified a great stock for an option trade but then capped the upside on the trade by using an advanced strategy such as the bull call spread. Don't let your ego get in the way of using these basic strategies. They can be every bit as effective and profitable as the advanced strategies.

Along similar lines, some traders may think that the basic strategies don't look sophisticated enough or that if they use them, they'll be unable to tell a story to their friends or golf buddies about how smart they are. Remember that you are not in the "looking sophisticated business" but rather in the "making money business." If you want to look sophisticated, buy a tuxedo. You do not earn style points in the stock and options markets. The only barometer of success is making a profitable trade; follow the money, not your ego. Find the strategy that's right for the situation—sometimes it's a basic strategy and sometimes it's a more advanced one—and then use it.

Avoid the trap of thinking that the basic strategies are inferior or uncool because they're basic. Sometimes they're the right strategy for the trading setup that you're seeing and want to capitalize on, and you'll need to be able to identify that. Now on to the advanced strategies.

Chapter 5

Intermediate and Advanced Options Strategies

This chapter (and the next two) describe multipart options strategies—those that combine multiple elements into a single trade. This chapter focuses on strategies that use two components, either a stock and an option or a combination of two options. The strategies allow you to profit in specific scenarios, and they're generally directional wagers on the performance of the underlying asset, meaning that they profit if the stock moves one way or the other. But sometimes they're bidirectional bets, so they profit if the stock moves in either direction, or they even profit if the stock doesn't move much at all.

The strategies here serve many different purposes: Some are used to generate income, some are used as insurance to protect a stock position that could rise, and others can be used to multiply your money many times over. Several of these strategies are useful for risk-averse investors looking to generate additional income and may be popular with retirees or others looking for cash flow.

COVERED CALL

Generate Income with a Safer Strategy

The covered call takes a riskier basic options strategy—the short call—and pairs it with a stock position to create a relatively safe and popular intermediate strategy. In a covered call, you sell a call option for every 100 shares of stock owned. In effect, the covered call trades the stock's upside above the strike price until the option's expiration in exchange for a cash payment today.

The potential upside on this strategy is the premium received from selling the call and perhaps a capital gain, while the downside can vary, depending on the performance of the stock. However, by owning the underlying stock, you hedge a key risk of the short call, namely, the potential loss if the stock moves significantly higher.

WHEN TO USE THE COVERED CALL

The covered call is a useful strategy when you want to own the stock over a longer period, but don't expect the underlying stock to move much higher until the call's expiration. You'll collect the premium up front, and if the stock remains below the call's strike price at expiration, you keep the full premium and the call is unlikely to be exercised, meaning you'll continue to hold the stock. Even if the stock rises above the strike and is called away, you're protected by the stock, which rises to offset the loss on the call option. The covered call can be a valuable strategy to generate income from a long-term holding that may or may not already pay a dividend. However, if the call were exercised and consequently selling the stock would create burdensome tax consequences, perhaps because of a large potential capital gain, the covered call may not be an attractive strategy. This kind of external consideration can have important ramifications on how you use this strategy.

A Popular Strategy for Income

The ability to generate income with limited risk makes the covered call somewhat more popular with retirees and others who have tax-advantaged retirement accounts, where they can delay or even entirely avoid the tax impact of the income and a potential capital gain.

HOW TO MODIFY
THE COVERED CALL

You can modify the strikes on the covered call to adjust your risk and return, reducing the likelihood that your stock will be called in exchange for a lower up-front premium or trade more risk for more premium. Selling an in-the-money call means that the stock will be called away unless the stock falls below the strike by the option's expiration. In exchange, you get a larger premium. In contrast, selling an out-of-the-money call earns a much lower premium with a lower chance that the stock will exceed the strike price by expiration, but also offers the potential for a capital gain up to the strike price.

THE PROFIT POTENTIAL OF A COVERED CALL

The profit potential of a covered call has two components—the performance of the stock and that of the short call—and the total profit on the strategy is the combination of those two. During the life of the strategy, you bear all the downside of the stock, and the only upsides are the call's premium and any upside between the stock price and the strike price. You can run through the following examples at various risk levels to see how it works.

Stock XYZ is trading for $50 per share, and you think it's an interesting long-term stock, though it looks a little pricey now. You can sell a call with a strike of $52.50 expiring in four months for $2.50. Here's the profit at various stock prices at expiration.

The covered call

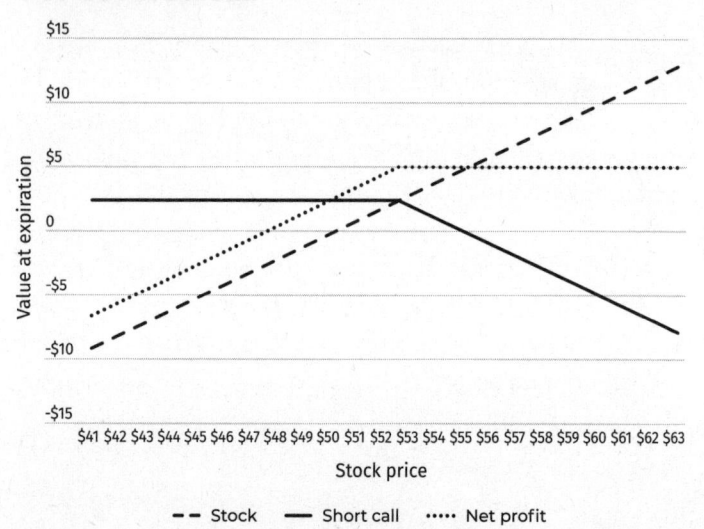

- The point of maximum profit occurs at the strike price, where you continue to hold the stock, enjoying its rise from $50 to $52.50, and the short call expires worthless. The total gain is $5 per share. Above this price, the profit flatlines, as you can see in the graph.
- The trade starts to lose money on a net basis if the stock falls below $47.50, or the stock price minus the premium of $2.50.
- Above the strike of $52.50, the stock is called away, and you keep the $2.50 premium and record an incremental capital gain on the stock of $2.50, or the $52.50 sale price minus the $50 current price. However, you don't make money on the stock that you would have made if the call had not been sold. Above $55 (the strike plus the premium), you would have made more money by not using a covered call.

The covered call trades the potential upside on the stock for an up-front payment today. If the stock doesn't reach the strike by expiration, you keep the full premium. But you must also endure any short-term downside on the stock, a risk that may be worthwhile if the stock is likely to be a strong long-term performer. If the stock rises past the strike, you lose out on money that you would have otherwise made without the short call. In this case, the loss on the short call is hedged and completely offset by the stock.

WHAT TO WATCH FOR

The covered call can feel a little more riskless than it actually is. The stock hedges any potential loss from the short call, so if the stock soars, the loss may not feel like it's coming out of your pocket, exactly. But that's just mental gymnastics. In the example just described, if the stock closed expiration at $62, you would have lost $7 per share that otherwise would have been gained, if not for the covered call. It's a real loss that would not have occurred but for selling the call.

So, when setting up a covered call, you should carefully consider the consequences if the stock is called from you or not. Will you be satisfied with the net sales price even if the stock soars and you're left out? The sale of stock via an exercised call is still taxable; does that create a burden, or should the stock not be sold at all? Tax-advantaged accounts shield the immediate tax consequences of covered calls—both the income and the capital gain—making the strategy more popular in these accounts. Finally, it's important to remember that you're tying your hands (somewhat) during the duration of the call, even if you could close out the transaction for some cost. You're agreeing to bear the downside risk on the stock for the length of the strategy rather than sell it, so you want to be comfortable with this risk if you set up a covered call. In other words, the stock should be something you're comfortable owning longer.

PROTECTIVE PUT

The protective put does what its name suggests—protect an existing position if it declines in value, much like insurance. To set up a protective put, you purchase a put for every 100 shares of the underlying stock. A similar strategy called the married put sets up the trade by buying the stock and the put at the same time but otherwise functions the same.

The potential upside on this strategy is uncapped, since the stock can rise many times in value, while the downside is limited due to the long put but only during the life of the option. If you want to offset the full decline in the stock, the strategy uses a more expensive at-the-money put, or you can purchase a cheaper out-of-the-money put and absorb some loss before the insurance kicks in.

WHEN TO USE THE PROTECTIVE PUT

The goal of a protective put is to allow you to continue owning the stock without enduring a decline in the stock. For this options strategy to make sense, you must expect the stock to rise over time, particularly during the life of the option, but foresee the potential for the stock to fall, perhaps due to a short-term event. So, the strategy allows you to profit if the stock rises but covers the downside if it doesn't. You don't use this strategy on stocks that you expect to fall over time, in which case it would make sense to sell the stock and then simply buy a put.

HOW TO MODIFY THE PROTECTIVE PUT

You can modify the strike price and expiration on the protective put to change its cost and adjust how much loss you're willing to absorb before the "insurance" begins covering you and for how long. For example, you could buy a put that is 7%–10% below the current stock price if you want to take that loss in exchange for a cheaper premium. If you need the put for a longer period, then you can extend the duration of the contract at greater expense. But remember that the point of this put is that it protects against loss on a stock that you expect to go up over time. So, paying a higher premium for a longer expiration may not be worth it.

THE PROFIT POTENTIAL OF A PROTECTIVE PUT

The total return of the strategy relies on the performance of the put as well as that of the stock. If the stock rises by expiration, it offsets the cost of the put and makes the put worthless, assuming the stock is above the strike price. If the stock falls, the put becomes more valuable and offsets the stock's decline, but it's important to factor in the put's cost to get an idea of the strategy's all-in cost and potential returns.

Stock XYZ is trading at $50 per share, and research suggests that the stock should rise, but an upcoming earnings report may send the stock lower for a while. You own 100 shares already, so you can set up a protective put with a $50 strike expiring in two months for $1.25, covering the period where you think the stock may move lower. Here's the profit at various stock prices at expiration.

The protective put

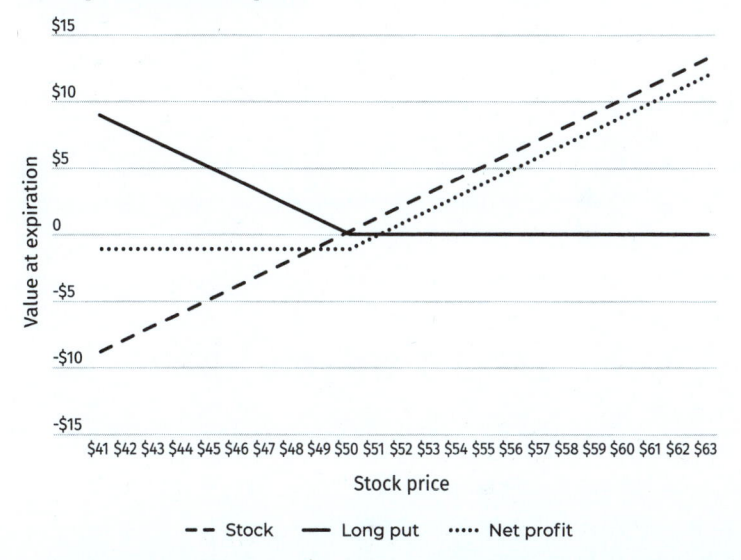

- The option begins to turn a profit at $48.75, or the strike price minus the $1.25 cost. Every subsequent $1 fall in the stock is directly and fully offset by the increase in the long put's value until expiration. As a whole, the stock and options position are exposed to, at most, this $1.25 loss for the duration of the contract.
- If the stock rises by expiration, you keep any gain, and the put expires worthless. The stock could continue rising with no limit to the potential upside. However, the total profit on the trade is offset by the $1.25 cost of the put. If the stock closes expiration at $55, the net profit is $3.75, or the stock's $5 gain minus the $1.25 option cost.

If you were willing to bear a further loss, the trade could be set up with a long put with a $45 strike at a lower cost, say, $0.50. You would eat any loss between $45 and $50—much like an insurance deductible—and then the put would begin protecting the position from $45. The most you would lose would be $5.50, or the $5 capital loss plus the $0.50 cost of the contract.

Options As Insurance

In setting up a protective put, you'll need to think about how much you need it, what losses it will offset, and how much you're willing to pay for it, much as you would for real insurance.

WHAT TO WATCH FOR

You need to believe that the stock will rise in value to justify adding the extra cost of the option. Unlike physical objects, a stock position can be relatively easy to exit, if you think the stock is about to be destroyed. You can't readily sell your house or car before a hurricane blows through your neighborhood.

It's also useful to understand that a protective put is the same as a long call at the same strike and expiration. That may sound counterintuitive, but it follows from the put-call parity rules laid out earlier in this book. It may be easier to understand if you consider the goal of a protective put: to allow you to profit on the rise of the stock. By purchasing the put, you're effectively trading away the risk of the stock falling until expiration, leaving only the stock's upside. In other words, you get only the upside exposure until expiration— which is effectively the same trade as a long call. So, if you wanted the same exposure without having to own the stock and buy the put, you could exit the stock position and instead simply buy a call.

That said, you may have other reasons to set up a protective put rather than selling the stock and buying a call. Substantial embedded capital gains on the stock could make it a nonstarter to liquidate the stock and buy an equivalent call due to a potential sizable tax bill.

SYNTHETIC LONG

Get a Stock's Returns with No Cash Up Front

The synthetic long replicates the return profile of owning the underlying asset directly. In a synthetic long—sometimes called a "syn long"—you buy a call and sell a put at the same strike price and expiration. This combination should mimic the performance of the underlying stock or fund for the limited duration of the option's lifetime.

The potential upside on this strategy is uncapped, while the downside is limited to the put's strike price plus any net debit or minus any net credit. A key advantage of a synthetic long is that you can set it up to require little, if any, capital, in contrast to owning the stock directly. Depending on the strategy's strike price, you may get paid to set up a synthetic long, though it's a riskier strategy than setting up an at-the-money or in-the-money synthetic long.

WHEN TO USE THE SYNTHETIC LONG

The synthetic long can be a useful strategy when you expect the stock to move significantly higher before the strategy's expiration. Since a synthetic long requires less capital than owning the stock directly, it can be useful when you have a limited bankroll. That said, remember that if the trade moves against you, you'll need the financial capacity to purchase the stock if it's put to you, either cash or margin capacity.

HOW TO MODIFY THE SYNTHETIC LONG

You can modify the strikes on the synthetic long to adjust your risk and return. If you want a riskier choice, move the strike price above the current stock price and receive a net credit. On the other hand, you can reduce your risk by moving the strike price below the current stock price and paying a net debit. Setting up a synthetic long with a strike that's higher than the current stock price means that the stock must move up before expiration or the short put will be exercised against you. In contrast, a synthetic long struck below the current stock price costs a net debit, but it reduces your risk since the put is out of the money. In a lower-risk scenario, the stock may fall somewhat by expiration without the put being exercised, though the synthetic long will lose some value.

Infinite Returns

The synthetic long allows you to literally generate infinite returns on your invested capital, which may not require any net cash investment, if the strategy is set up at the money. However, don't make the mistake of thinking this strategy is risk-free. You still assume the risk of the stock falling.

THE PROFIT POTENTIAL OF A SYNTHETIC LONG

The profit potential of a synthetic long has two parts—the performance of the long call and that of the short put. If the stock rises, the call becomes more valuable and the put less so. On the other hand, if the stock falls, the call becomes less valuable and the put creates a larger loss. Here are some examples to show how it works.

Stock XYZ is trading for $50 per share, and it looks like it can move up in the near term. You can set up a synthetic long with a $47.50 call expiring in six months for $4.50 and sell a $47.50 put for $2 with the same expiration. The net debit for this trade is $2.50, which is exactly the difference between the stock price and the strike price of the synthetic long. Here's the profit at various stock prices at expiration.

The synthetic long

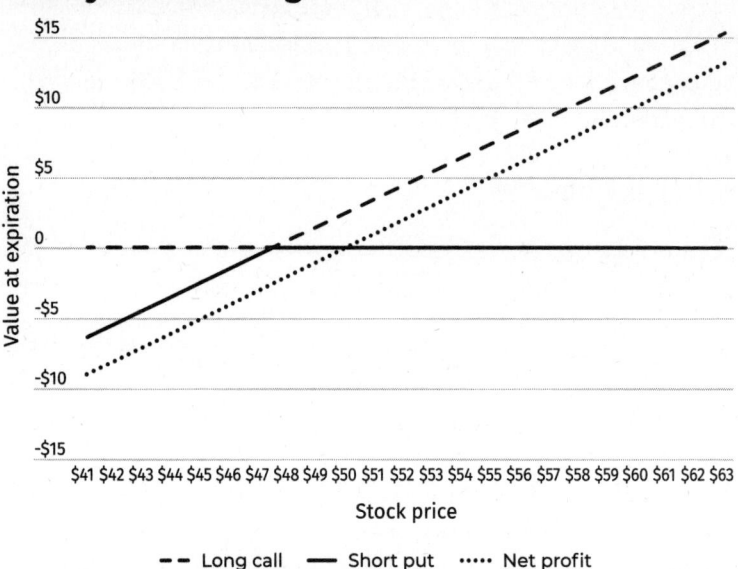

- The position breaks even at $50, or the strike price plus the net debit of $2.50, and the return profile looks like the stock's at expiration. If the stock's profit line were shown on the graph, it would be superimposed right on the existing net profit line.

- If the stock finishes expiration below $47.50, the put is exercised, and you must buy the stock at $47.50.
- Every $1 rise in the stock at expiration results in a $1 increase in the trade's profit, while every $1 fall in the stock at expiration results in a $1 decrease in the trade's profit—the same as if you owned the stock.

By adjusting the strikes on the synthetic long, you can receive a net credit, pay a net debit, or make a more-or-less even trade of a call for a put. A higher-risk trade may offer a net credit up front, with you bearing increased risk that the short put will be exercised. In contrast, a lower-risk trade may require you to put up some money but may allow the stock to fall somewhat before the put will be exercised.

WHAT TO WATCH FOR

If you're more aggressively bullish, you can modify a synthetic long to pay off even more favorably if you're right. The strategy here is to set up a synthetic long well above the current stock price, resulting in a net credit. That net credit is then used to purchase another call, leveraging the trade to the upside. For example, you set up a syn long at a higher strike price and receive a $5 credit for the short put, while the corresponding long call costs $2.50. You then purchase two calls for every short put, meaning the profit could soar once the stock reaches the strike price. If you're still more aggressive and confident in your analysis, you could take an even more leveraged position of three times or more. This modification may be particularly attractive using long-term options that give the stock time to rise above the strike and the thesis time to play out.

A two-legged position like the synthetic long can also allow you to "leg out" of a trade, especially if it moves favorably early on. If the stock moves higher, you can decide whether it's an attractive time to repurchase the short put and close out that leg, eliminating the downside risk and the associated margin capacity that's tied up because of it. Then you'll be left with only a long call. But if the chances of the stock falling and the put going in the money are low, it may make little sense to close the put.

The short put has the potential to be exercised early if it's deep in the money and has little time value remaining, ending the strategy early.

SYNTHETIC SHORT

Short a Stock with No Up-Front Cash

The synthetic short does what a synthetic long does but in reverse—it replicates the return profile of short-selling the underlying asset directly. In a synthetic short—or "syn short"—you sell a call and buy a put at the same strike price and expiration. This combo should mirror the performance of the underlying stock or fund for the duration of the option's lifetime.

The potential upside on this strategy is capped at the strike price of the long put plus any net premium received or minus any net premium paid, but it can still return many times the original investment. The downside is uncapped, due to the short call. A key advantage of the synthetic short is that you can set it up to require little, if any, capital; this means you needn't borrow on margin, as you would for a regular short stock position.

WHEN TO USE THE SYNTHETIC SHORT

As the inverse of the synthetic long, the synthetic short is useful when you expect the stock to fall before the option's expiration. A synthetic short requires less capital than shorting the stock directly, and you can set it up without borrowing from your broker, as you would need to do with a regular short sale. However, you'll need the financial capacity to settle the trade if the stock rises and someone exercises the call and forces you to deliver the underlying stock.

HOW TO MODIFY THE SYNTHETIC SHORT

You can modify the strikes on the synthetic short to adjust your risk and return, according to your preferences. As a base case, you can set up a synthetic short with a strike at the current stock price. If you want a riskier choice, move the strike price below the current stock price and receive a net credit. If you want less risk, you can move the strike price above the current stock price and pay a net debit. Setting up the synthetic short with a strike price below the stock price means the stock must move lower before expiration or the short call will be exercised against you. On the flip side, a synthetic short set up above the current stock price costs a net debit but reduces risk because the stock is already below the strike price. If the trade is set up with the strike price above the stock price, the stock may rise somewhat (up to the strike price) by expiration without the call being exercised, though the synthetic short will decline in value.

Regardless of the strategy's strike price, the overall return profile is the same at each stock price. The difference is whether you pay or get paid to take more risk, by assuming a strike price that is higher or lower than the current stock price. A riskier trade (at a lower strike) enjoys a net credit, while a safer trade (at a higher strike) pays a net debit.

Shorting Without Borrowing

Like the synthetic long, the synthetic short lets you generate an infinite return on invested capital, because it may require no net investment if this strategy is set up at the current stock price. But it's not risk-free, since the synthetic short leaves you with an unhedged short call hanging out there.

THE PROFIT POTENTIAL OF A SYNTHETIC SHORT

The return on the synthetic short relies on the performance of both options. If the stock falls, the put becomes valuable and the call less valuable, and vice versa, if the stock rises. Consider this example to see how it works.

Stock XYZ is trading at $50 per share, and your research suggests that the stock should fall soon. You decide to set up a synthetic short with a $50 call expiring in six months for $2.50 and a $50 put for $2.50 with the same expiration. The premiums offset one another, leaving you with no net cost. Here's the profit at various stock prices at expiration.

The synthetic short

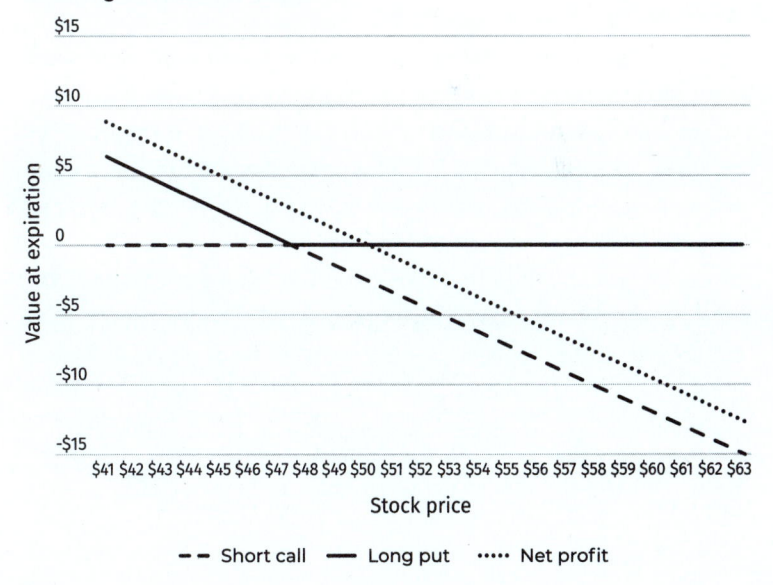

- The strategy breaks even at $50, and the return profile looks like the stock's at the strategy's expiration. As shown in the net profit line in the graphic, each $1 rise in the stock at expiration results in a $1 decline in the trade's profit, and each $1 fall in the stock results in a $1 increase in profit—exactly the profit if you short-sold the stock directly.
- If the stock finishes expiration below $50, the put is in the money and you should exercise the option. Below $50, the call expires worthless.
- If the stock finishes expiration above $50, the call is in the money and will be exercised, with you being forced to deliver the stock. Above $50, the put expires worthless.

WHAT TO WATCH FOR

If you're aggressively bearish, you could set up an even more leveraged trade by taking a net credit and buying more puts, potentially multiplying your returns even more, if you're right. For example, you could set up the synthetic short well below the current stock price and then use the extra cash to buy an additional put. If you set up a synthetic short at a lower strike price and receive a $6 premium for the short call while the corresponding long put costs $3, you could buy two long puts for every short call. The position's profit will double for any move below the strike price. If you're still more aggressive and confident that the stock will fall, you could set up positions that are even more leveraged with a much lower strike price. Long-term options can help with these trades, since they give time for the investment thesis to play out, if it's correct.

You can "leg out" of the synthetic short early, especially if it moves in a favorable direction early on. For example, if the stock moves lower, you can choose whether it's a good time to buy back the short call and close out that leg of the trade, if at all. This move eliminates the risk of the stock rising and frees up the related margin capacity that's tied up, and you'll be left with only a long put. If it's unlikely that the stock rises again before expiration, it may make little sense to do this.

The short call may be exercised early if it's deep in the money and has little time value remaining, ending the strategy early.

LONG STRADDLE

Profit Whichever Way a Stock Moves

The long straddle is a wager that a stock will move significantly in one direction or the other, and the strategy offers a bidirectional play on that move, regardless of the move. In a long straddle, you buy a call as well as a put at the same strike price and the same expiration, typically at-the-money options.

The potential upside on this strategy is high, while the downside is limited to the price paid for the options. Either leg can return many times its value, though only one leg at most can be in the money at expiration. If the stock continues rising, the long call has no limit to the upside, while the long put's upside is capped at the total value of the strike price, though that may be multiples of the investment.

WHEN TO USE THE LONG STRADDLE

The long straddle could be an effective strategy when you expect a large move in the stock by expiration but can't predict which direction it may go. For example, it might be an attractive strategy if a company is awaiting big news—say, approval of a key drug—that could make or break the company's fortunes. The high setup cost here means that it should be used selectively, including how long the strategy is in force. Setting up a long straddle requires twice the up-front capital of a one-way long position, but it pays out only at the same rate as a one-way strategy. This disadvantage means that you really need a stock that is likely to make a big move to offset the cost of the unprofitable leg. However, in the short term, this strategy could benefit from an increase in volatility. So, even if the stock doesn't move as expected, an increase in volatility could help both legs of the trade.

Profit on Any Stock Move

With two long legs, this strategy is besieged on both sides by time, which is working twice as hard against this trade. This drawback means that you should ensure this strategy is the right one.

HOW TO MODIFY THE LONG STRADDLE

A long straddle is usually made at or near the money using the nearest strike price. The stock may fall nearly in the middle of two strike prices, depending on the intervals between strikes, which may be as wide as $5, though they're typically $2.50 or even $1. So, modifications to the long straddle commonly consist in changing the duration of the strategy rather than in adjusting the strikes, unlike in other options strategies.

As you're setting up a straddle, it's important that it covers the period where you expect the stock move to occur, or you'll end up paying for nothing. Extending a straddle's duration costs money on both sides, so you pay twice as much. While it could make sense to wait closer to the expected event, options prices may increase further on implied volatility. You'll want to balance this time element carefully.

THE PROFIT POTENTIAL OF A LONG STRADDLE

The return on the straddle depends on the performance of both options, though only one of them will drive your profit, with the other expiring worthless if held to expiration. If the stock rises significantly, the call becomes more valuable and the put expires. If the stock falls, the put becomes more valuable, while the call expires worthless. But if the stock doesn't move much at all, both options end up losing most of their value—the worst outcome for the long straddle.

Stock XYZ is priced at $50 per share, and it's awaiting FDA approval of a new drug that could make or break the company in the next few months. You decide to set up a long straddle at $50 for three months. The call costs $5 and the put costs $5, so it costs a net $10 to set up. Here's the profit at various stock prices at expiration.

The long straddle

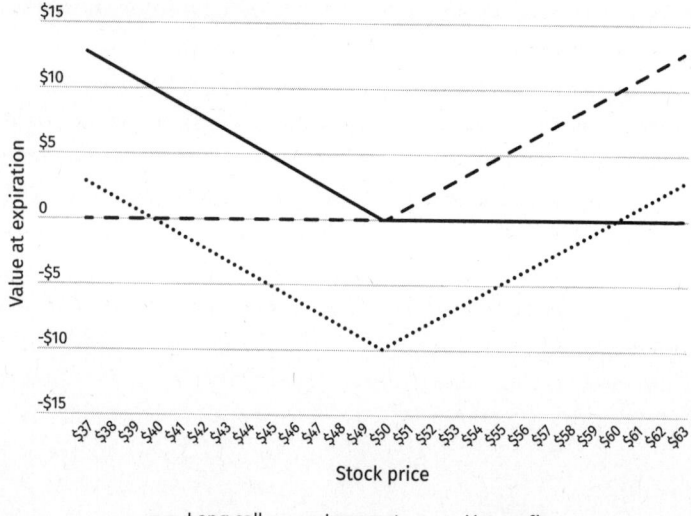

Stock price

- - Long call   —— Long put   ····· Net profit

- The whole strategy breaks even at $40 and $60, or the strike price plus and minus the cost of the premiums together. At any stock price between $40 and $60 at expiration, the long straddle is a net loser, though either the call or put will retain some value (except if the stock closes expiration at $50) and can be sold or exercised, if it makes sense.
- The put alone breaks even below $45, while the call alone breaks even above $55. But those outcomes are mutually exclusive, at least at expiration.
- In this example, the strategy can return many times its cost if the stock moves higher. If the stock moved to $150, the profit would be $90. In this situation, the call would be worth $100, the put would be worth nothing, and the setup cost $10. But the potential profit on the put is capped at $40, in the case that the stock goes to $0. Then the put would be worth $50, the call nothing, and the setup cost $10.

You need a substantial move to make setting up the long straddle worthwhile, even if the options are more moderately priced than in this example. If the stock moves lower, the potential gain—a maximum of just $40—may not be worth setting it up. However, if the stock moves higher, the potential upside is much greater. A similar strategy called the strangle (explained later) may reduce your setup costs, however, and make a bidirectional wager more feasible.

WHAT TO WATCH FOR

The downside of the long straddle is—to paraphrase great ad executive John Wanamaker—that half of your cost is wasted; you just don't know which half. The trade's bidirectional nature means that at most only one of the two options can be in the money when the strategy expires, though you'll still have to buy both, entailing a significant outlay. Worse, if the stock doesn't move much—that is, if it stays near the strike price—both options lose most of their value, if not all, at expiration.

It's important to remember that options price-in expected volatility, since traders want to be paid for the risks they're running. If traders see the risk approaching, they're going to start pricing it in. So, an aggressive trader may decide to make this trade expecting that implied volatility increases, raising the price of both options, rather than as a play on the actual outcome of the news.

If the stock moves substantially before the news is announced and a good amount of time remains, you have choices. It might make sense to close the profitable leg while you can and reduce risk, especially if you expect the stock may move back toward the strike. Depending on the price of the unprofitable leg and the remaining time to expiration, you may consider holding or selling for some cash while you can.

SHORT STRADDLE

Profit from a Stock Going Nowhere

The elements that make the long straddle tough may make the short straddle easier. The short straddle is the direct opposite, offering a wager that the stock will not move much one way or the other by expiration. In a short straddle, you sell a call as well as a put at the same strike price and the same expiration, usually at the money.

This strategy's maximum potential upside is capped at the premiums received up front, and the best-case scenario is that the stock finishes right at the strike price, allowing you to capture all, or nearly all, of both premiums. Time works in the favor of this strategy, as each day it tends to decrease the value of both options. The maximum downside on the short straddle is theoretically unlimited.

WHEN TO USE THE SHORT STRADDLE

The short straddle can be an attractive strategy when you expect the stock to not move much by the options' expiration. Volatile stocks offer higher premiums because of their potential to move more. However, you could set up a short straddle on a steadier stock and receive an attractive premium overall, despite the lower volatility, since the trade involves selling two options and delivers twice the up-front premium as setting up a one-directional position. The short straddle may be attractive if you expect a stock's implied volatility to decline during the trade's lifetime. Even a modest decline in implied volatility may see the short straddle benefit, and it does so on both legs of the trade. With two short options and the risk they entail, a short straddle requires substantial marginable equity to set up.

As you're setting up short straddles, you'll need to pay attention to key events—earnings, a big company announcement, and other such market-moving news—to be sure you're being compensated enough for the potential risks. Shorter-term short straddles may help here.

HOW TO MODIFY THE SHORT STRADDLE

A short straddle is usually made at or near the money. Of course, a stock is not always right at an available strike price, so you may need to select the closest available strike. Modifications to the short straddle consist more of changing its duration than adjusting the strikes, since the trade works bidirectionally, unlike basic options strategies. Setting up a short straddle with a shorter duration—say, less than two months—may be more attractive than a longer-duration one. Time value tends to be more expensive on a per-day basis for shorter-term contracts than for longer-term contracts, and time value decays faster in the last two months or so of its lifetime—both attractive traits for short positions.

THE PROFIT POTENTIAL OF A SHORT STRADDLE

The return on the short straddle depends on both legs, but the trade's bidirectional nature means that you're likely to get most or all the value out of at least one of the legs. So, only one leg at most will possibly wind up in the money, while the other ends up worthless. But if the stock moves a little in one direction by expiration, you may end up with one leg expiring worthless and the other leg being net profitable for you even if it's still in the money. So, you're not likely to earn the whole net credit when you set up this trade and will most probably give some back. But in the best-case scenario the stock ends right at the strike price at expiration, allowing you to keep the full premium on both legs.

Stock XYZ is priced at $50 per share, and it has just reported earnings and has nothing on the horizon for the next two months. You decide to set up a short straddle at $50 for two months. The call pays $3 and the put pays $3, so it provides a net $6 to set up. Here's the profit at various stock prices at expiration.

The short straddle

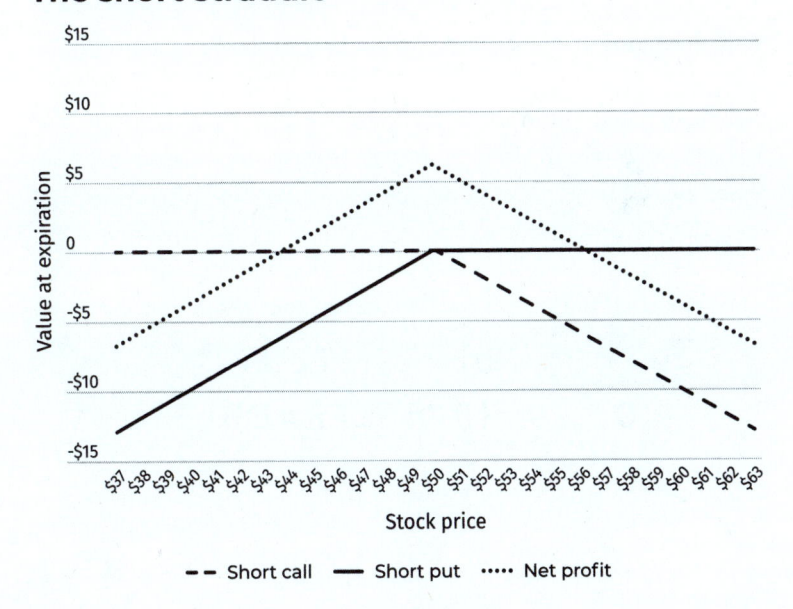

- This strategy breaks even at $44 and $56, or the strike price plus and minus the total premium received. Between the stock prices of $44 and $56, the short straddle is a net winner, though either the call or put may retain some value (except at a stock price of $50) and can be repurchased, or it may be exercised against you.
- The put breaks even at $47, while the call breaks even at $53. While generally those outcomes are mutually exclusive, the stock may fluctuate enough during the options' lifetime that it's possible for one or both options to be exercised unfavorably.
- The maximum return on the short straddle is the premiums received up front, $6 here, and only if the stock finishes expiration at $50. If the stock races higher to $125, the short straddle loses a net $69. The call is worth $75, the put is worth nothing, and the loss is offset by the $6 in premiums. The maximum loss on the put is $44, if the stock goes to $0. Here the put would be worth $50, the call expires worthless, and they're offset by the $6 in premiums.

This strategy's benefit is that the stock must move substantially to overcome the up-front payment, though you can get hit from either direction. The short straddle wins if the stock simply finishes near the strategy's strike price, with most of the options' value gone. More likely, at least one of the legs retains some value and will need to be closed. If the option is in the money near expiration, it may be exercised, and you'll need to deliver the stock (for calls) at the strike or buy the stock (for puts).

WHAT TO WATCH FOR

With short options it can make sense to close the position when you've captured most of the value rather than riding out the trade to expiration and risk a last-minute move in the stock. As you near expiration, the risk of an in-the-money option being exercised increases, though only one option is in the money at any time.

With this type of multi-leg trade it can make sense to "leg out" if it's cheap to do so. If the stock moves sharply, you could close out the cheaper leg if there's a chance that the stock could reverse and make this leg worth much more. But it may make more sense to let that option expire worthless and capture the full premium, using that extra cash to offset what may be the losing leg of the trade. You'll have to judge the risk and reward.

LONG STRANGLE

The long strangle is much like the long straddle and profits in similar circumstances: if the stock moves significantly higher or lower. In a long strangle, you buy a call and a put at different strike prices—a put below the current stock price and a call above it—but at the same expiration. The long strangle is generally cheaper to set up than a long straddle because of the "hole" in the middle of the strikes, but it requires an even larger move from the stock to make it profitable.

The potential upside on the long strangle is unlimited, and the downside is limited to the premiums paid for the options. The long positions can return multiples of their cost, though only one can be in the money at expiration, and it's possible that both expire worthless.

WHEN TO USE THE LONG STRANGLE

Like the long straddle, the long strangle can be an effective strategy when you expect the stock to move a lot by expiration but are unable to determine in which direction. If a company is awaiting make-or-break news, the long strangle may be a good pick. Because it buys out-of-the-money options, the stock needs to move significantly to make the strategy worthwhile. Setting up a long strangle requires twice the premium of a one-way long position, though it only pays at most on one leg of the trade, if that. So, it's a hurdle for this strategy to become profitable and offset the costs of the two premiums and for it to escape the gap in coverage in the strangle's middle.

HOW TO MODIFY THE LONG STRANGLE

Modifications to the long strangle include adjusting the strikes based on your expectations of the stock's movement. A long strangle is often created with options that are one or two strikes away from—both above and below—the current stock price. Higher-priced stocks outside the typical $20–$100 trading range could see a long strangle set up at wider strikes, though at a similar percentage above and below the current stock price, say, 5%–10%. You could move the strikes further away from the current stock price to reduce the capital required. But this would be at the higher risk of the stock not moving sufficiently to result in a profitable trade.

The long strangle must cover the period when you expect the stock's move to occur. Extending the expiration of the trade costs further money on both sides of the strategy. If you wait until closer to the event, you may pay higher prices based on higher expectations of volatility. So, timing the purchase and expiration of the long strangle should be weighed carefully.

THE PROFIT POTENTIAL
OF A LONG STRANGLE

The return on the strangle relies on the performance of both options, and at least one should expire worthless with the other driving any incremental profit, if any. If the stock rises a lot, the call becomes more valuable and the put becomes worthless at expiration. If the stock falls a lot, the put becomes more valuable and the call expires worthless. However, if the stock stays between the two strike prices at expiration, both options expire worthless—a key difference between the long strangle and the long straddle.

Use the same example from the straddle section and set up a long strangle instead. Stock XYZ is priced at $50, and it's awaiting FDA approval of a new drug that could make or break the company in the next few months. You can set up a long strangle at $45 and $55 for three months. The call costs $2.50 and the put costs $2.50, or a net $5. Here's the profit at various stock prices at expiration.

The long strangle

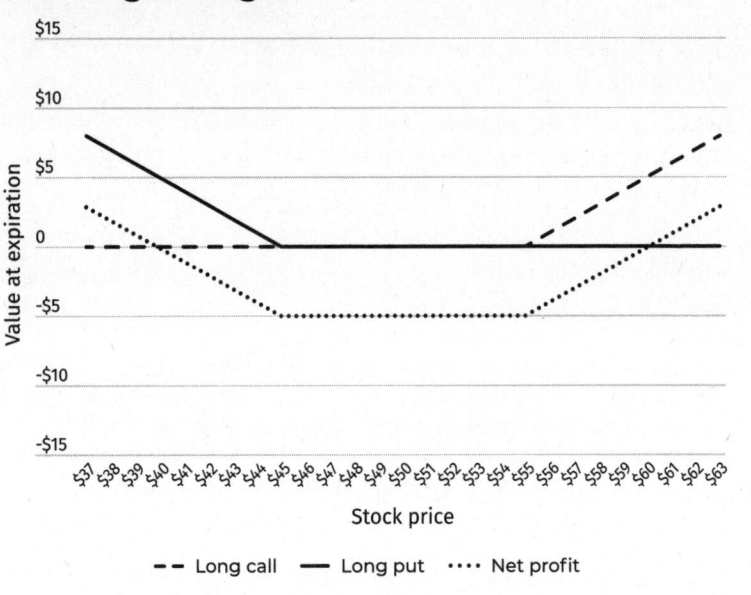

- This strategy breaks even at $40 and $60, or the call and put strikes plus and minus the total premium. At any price between $40 and $60, the long strangle is a net loser, though either the call or put could be in the money or even be profitable by itself and can be sold or otherwise exercised. If the stock finishes between the two strikes, both options expire worthless.

- The put by itself breaks even at $42.50, or the $45 strike price minus the $2.50 premium. The call by itself breaks even at $57.50, or the $55 strike plus the $2.50 premium. These outcomes are mutually exclusive, at least at expiration.
- The strategy can return multiples of the premium paid. If the stock climbed to $150, the profit would be $90. The call would be worth $95, the put would be worthless, and the setup cost $5. However, the potential profit if the stock falls is capped at $40, assuming the stock goes to $0. In this situation, the put is worth $45, the call is worthless, and the setup cost $5.

As in the long straddle, you need a substantial stock move to make the long strangle profitable. And compared to that strategy, with the long strangle you exchange that gaping hole in the middle of the strategy—$45–$55—for a lower up-front premium cost.

WHAT TO WATCH FOR

An aggressive trader may use any short-term increase in premiums due to a rise in implied volatility as an opportunity to close out one or both legs of this trade rather than waiting for news. Time hits the price on both legs, so this strategy needs volatility to ramp up quickly to make it a profitable gambit.

If the stock makes a big move before the potential news and a lot of time remains, you have choices to make. You could close a profitable leg and reduce the overall risk, particularly if the stock may drift back to the price where you set up the strategy. You'll need to balance the potential of the legs against their remaining time value to see whether it's worth holding or selling while you can.

The downside of the long strangle is that at most only one of the two legs of this trade will be profitable at expiration, though you'll still need to buy both to set up this bidirectional trade. The long strangle leaves a hole both above and below the current stock price, meaning that, if the stock stays within this gap, both options will expire worthless.

SHORT STRANGLE

Generate Income on a Stagnant Stock

The short strangle can benefit from some disadvantageous aspects of the long strangle. In a short strangle, you sell a call and a put at different strike prices—a put below the current stock price and a call above it—but at the same expiration. The short strangle provides a lower up-front payment than a short straddle due to the wider range of strikes and the gap in coverage between them, substantially increasing the chance that both legs of the strangle expire worthless.

The maximum potential upside on the short strangle is limited to the premiums received from the options at the start. Both options may end up expiring worthless, leaving you with the full premium as a profit. The maximum downside on the short strangle is literally uncapped, since one leg is an uncovered call, which can rise if the stock itself rises. If the stock falls substantially, however, this strategy can also cost many multiples of the premium received as the put increases in value. However, fortunately, only one option in the strangle can be in the money at expiration.

WHEN TO USE THE SHORT STRANGLE

Like the short straddle, the short strangle can be an effective strategy if you expect a stock to remain close to its current price until the strategy's expiration. The short strangle may be an attractive strategy to take advantage of higher option prices due to a stock's high implied volatility, if you expect its actual volatility to decline during the life of the strategy. However, in the short term, this strategy could be hurt by an increase in volatility, which could push up the price of both options. With two short options and their potential risks, a short strangle requires a lot of marginable equity to set up.

HOW TO MODIFY THE SHORT STRANGLE

A short strangle is often set up with options that are one or two strikes away from the current stock price, both above and below it. So, you may set up strikes on the call and put legs that are $2.50 or $5 on either side of the current stock price, allowing the stock to move some while still generating potentially attractive premiums. Options on higher-priced stocks outside the typical stock's trading range of $20–$100 could be set up at a similar percentage range, perhaps 5%–10% above and below the current stock price, depending on your expectations.

The strangle could be modified by adjusting the strikes based on how you expect the stock to act. Wider strikes give the stock more room to move without going into the money but offer a lower payout than a tighter strangle and may be worthwhile, depending on the expected volatility. You could also extend the expiration of the strategy to capture a larger premium, though you may be able to set up this strategy repeatedly for shorter durations and reap more total premiums.

THE PROFIT POTENTIAL OF A SHORT STRANGLE

The return on the short strangle depends on the strikes and expiration, but it's always limited to the premiums received up front. If the stock rises a lot, the call becomes more costly and the put becomes worthless at expiration. If the stock falls a lot, the put becomes more costly and the call expires worthless. At least one option should always expire worthless, leaving you with a full profit on that side of the trade. But if the stock closes expiration between the two strikes, both legs expire worthless, and you can keep the premium from both sides.

Consider an example of how to set up a short strangle. Stock XYZ is priced at $50 per share, and it's about to report earnings, which you think will leave the stock flat for the next few months. You decide to set up a short strangle at $45 and $55 for three months. The call pays $3 and the put pays $3, so it offers a net $6 to set up. Here's the profit at various stock prices at expiration.

The short strangle

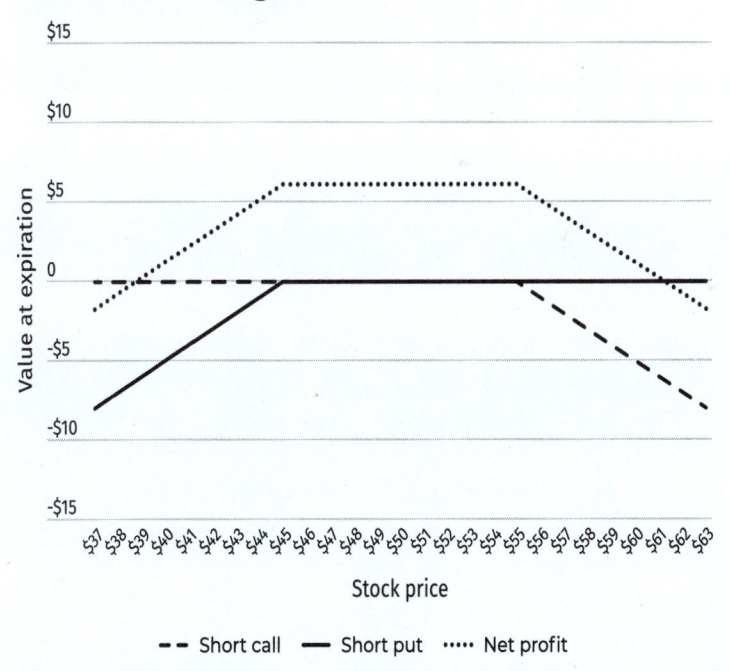

Stock price

- - Short call — Short put ••••• Net profit

- This strategy breaks even at $39 and $61, or the two strikes plus and minus the total premium. At any stock price between $39 and $61, the short strangle is a net winner, though either the call (above $55) or put (below $45) could expire in the money and be exercised. And if the stock finishes between the two strikes, $45–$55, both options expire worthless, and you keep the total premium.
- The put individually breaks even at $42, or the $45 strike price less the $3 premium. The call individually breaks even at $58, or the $55 strike plus the $3 premium. These outcomes are mutually exclusive, at least at expiration.
- The potential loss on the short strangle is uncapped. If the stock climbed to $150, the loss would be $89. The call would be worth $95, the put would be worthless, and the premium paid $6. However, the potential loss if the stock falls is capped at $39, if the stock goes to $0. In this situation, the put is worth $45, the call is worthless, and the premium paid $6.

WHAT TO WATCH FOR

Setting up a short strangle offers twice the premium of an individual short position, with generally only one leg at most finishing in the money. In some cases, neither option may end up in the money. The double premiums allow the stock more room to fluctuate higher or lower before the strategy starts to lose money on a net basis. With two short positions, the short strangle benefits twice as much from time decay eating away at the value of the options, compared to a single-leg strategy.

If the stock moves significantly in either direction before expiration and it has a real possibility of moving back toward its original price, it could make sense to close out the low-cost end of the trade and remove all risk from that leg. Of course, this decision depends on the option's price.

The strategy could be hurt by an increase in implied volatility, especially early on, raising the price of both options. But time works in your favor here, whittling down the price on both legs.

COLLAR

Protect Your Downside Without Giving Away All Upside

The collar does what its name suggests—collars a stock position from going much higher or much lower. In a collar, you sell an out-of-the-money call and buy an out-of-the-money put at the same expiration, and you also buy (or already own) the underlying stock. A collar functions like a covered call and a protective put in a single strategy, often with little or no cost. This strategy exchanges the stock's potential upside gain for downside protection, trading risk for risk.

The potential upside on the collar is limited to the difference between the call's strike and the stock price plus any net credit or minus any net debit. The potential downside is limited to the difference between the current stock price and the put's strike plus any net debit or minus any net credit. Both legs may end up expiring worthless if the stock stays near the current price at expiration.

WHEN TO USE THE COLLAR

The collar can be an effective strategy for a stock that may have some short-term downside but that you want to own over a longer term because of its potential to rise. For example, the collar could be suitable if a stock may dip after an earnings report, but you're bullish on its future. If structured well, a collar can still allow the stock to rise moderately, giving you some potential profit while partially offsetting a more serious decline in the stock, if that happens.

The collar can be a low-cost strategy, with the premium from the short call covering all (or almost all) of the cost of the long put, depending on how it's structured.

HOW TO MODIFY THE COLLAR

The key modification of the collar is setting the strikes wide enough so that they offer enough upside while covering the downside that you're looking to protect from. So, you may set up a collar that's 7%–10% above and below the current stock price, but you may "shade" the collar in one direction or the other. For example, if you want to leave more potential upside but curtail more downside, you could pay a larger net cost to set it up. Given that the strategy limits returns, you want the expirations to match your timing needs. The point here is protection, not profit. The collar is meant to protect the stock for a relatively short duration, perhaps over a specific event or period that may cause the stock to fall, though it could be extended for other specific purposes.

THE PROFIT POTENTIAL OF A COLLAR

The return on the collar depends significantly on the performance of the stock that's being collared. The strategy's total upside is capped when the stock hits the short call's strike price, at which point the call fully offsets the stock's rise, at expiration. This gain minus any net debit or plus any net credit is the most you can take away from this strategy. In this upside scenario the long put expires worthless.

And on the put side of the strategy, you bear any downside until the put's strike price, at which point the put begins offsetting the decline in the stock at expiration. In this downside scenario, the call expires worthless. Of course, the stock may finish expiration anywhere between these two strikes, with you having lost or gained some, depending on the exact strikes. Consider an example of how this works.

Stock XYZ is priced at $50 per share, and you expect the stock may fluctuate a lot when it reports earnings next month, though you're bullish on it for the next few years. You decide to set up a collar at $45 and $55 for two months. The call pays $1.50, while the put costs $1, for a net credit of $0.50. Here's the profit at various stock prices at expiration.

The collar

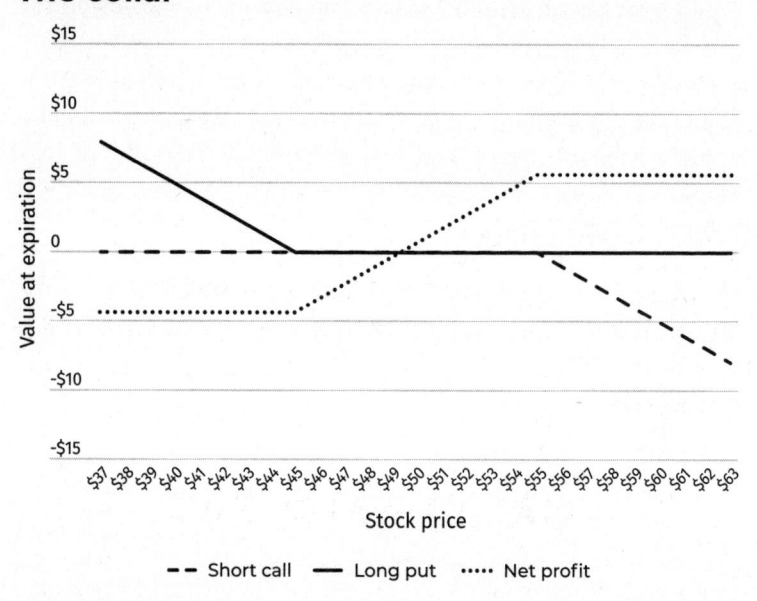

- This strategy breaks even at $49.50, or the current stock price minus the net credit of the strategy. Between $49.50 and $55, the strategy is profitable, though the profit tops out at $55, as the short call offsets any further stock gain, as measured at expiration. Above $55.50 (the call's strike price plus the $0.50 net credit) you would have made more money without setting up the collar, and the put expires worthless, since the stock is above the strike price at expiration.
- The protective put offers insurance, but you must endure the first $5 in downside (minus the offsetting $0.50 net credit) before that insurance reduces any loss, as measured at expiration. From there, the put fully offsets the downside at expiration. In this scenario, the call expires worthless, as the stock is below the $55 strike at expiration.
- If the stock finishes expiration anywhere between the two strikes, you enjoy the gain or suffer the loss as well as the net credit of $0.50. Both options expire worthless.

Collar, Collar Bills

The collar's purpose is to protect a potential long-term winner at not too great a cost, both in terms of the strategy's setup price and the cost of missing a rise in the stock. The strategy lets you enjoy some upside if you're willing to stomach some downside.

WHAT TO WATCH FOR

A collar may also require follow-up action after the end of the anticipated period of decline, especially if the strategy has significant time remaining on it. You may want to carefully decide whether it makes sense to continue holding the put after the big event, if the put is in the money or if significant time value remains on it. For example, if the stock falls after the event but you do not anticipate any further fall or even that the stock may rise again soon, it could make sense to sell the put and capture any available value.

Similarly, you may need to decide what to do with the short call, if significant time remains on it. In extreme scenarios, where the stock may rebound hard after a large initial drop, it could even make sense to close out the short call while it remains cheap, depending on exactly how cheap it is and how much time remains until expiration. But if the stock has not declined, you may need to close the collar, depending on the stock's anticipated movement. The existence of the short call may lead to missing out on a stock's gain if it's ready to run much higher.

Chapter 6

Spread Options Strategies

Spread options strategies are complex multi-leg strategies that tend to lessen risk while offering limited returns, and these strategies let you "carve out" the risk you want to own from a stock's return profile. With spreads, you can still make directional wagers on a stock's performance, but spreads can limit the potential downsides of these wagers by eliminating the "tail risk," the risk that a stock could soar or plummet and drive massive losses. So, spreads allow you to fine-tune the risk exposure you want, typically achieving more modest returns than basic options strategies but with more modest risks.

That's not to say that spreads offer only moderate returns, however. In fact, some spreads allow you to multiply your money many times and even turbocharge your returns, compared to the basic options strategies. However, spreads offer these benefits only within certain limits, which you establish when setting up the trade. On the flip side, spreads can generate limited income, compared to basic options strategies, while minimizing the risk.

PROS AND CONS OF SPREAD OPTIONS STRATEGIES

The Lower-Risk Way to Make Money

Spread options strategies are the province of the intermediate and advanced options trader, and these options offer knowledgeable traders a variety of benefits. However, spreads do come with some drawbacks compared to basic options strategies. Here are some of the key advantages and disadvantages.

ADVANTAGES OF SPREAD OPTIONS

Spread strategies offer several benefits for those who can use them effectively, including the following.

Fine-Tuned Risk-Taking

In a real sense, spread strategies are the epitome of options trading. Spreads let you narrow your exposure to certain types of risk and then you can buy and sell just that risk. With a basic options strategy, for example, you can own a stock's upside above $100 a share for six months. But a spread strategy can allow you to buy the part of that upside that you really want—say, from $100 to $120—and then sell the part you don't want, from $120 and up, all while reducing the impact of volatility and time decay. With spreads you can isolate and trade the risk that you really want to trade and minimize other uninteresting or non-lucrative risks.

Limited Risk

Spreads are hedged transactions because they set up two or more options that limit the risk and reward of the other options in the spread. Because of this hedge, these strategies typically limit how much you can lose, albeit at the cost of some maximum return. In contrast, when you sell a call or put, you could have nearly uncapped risk and lose many more times the premium you gain from the trade. With spreads, you can still lose more than you gain, but the loss is often limited to a manageable amount, and you have a firm idea of how much that amount is.

Reduced Net Investment and Turbocharged Gains

Spread strategies pair multiple contracts together, often two calls or two puts, and you're selling one while buying the other. Because of this structure, your net investment in a long spread is less than it would be with a basic options strategy. You're also getting less risk exposure for that lower up-front investment, so you're owning the risk you want to own. In a bull call spread, for example, you can buy a long call and then sell away risk above a certain level using a short call, leaving you with a lower net investment but the same total return up to the short call's strike. Since you're paying less to set up the spread, you lower your breakeven price and can turbocharge your percentage return up to the short strike, compared with a long call alone. In effect, the stock must move less for you to receive a more attractive gain, compared to a long call only.

DISADVANTAGES OF SPREAD OPTIONS

Spread strategies have downsides that you must understand before you begin trading them, including the following:

Higher Complexity

Spread strategies offer complexity from mildly more complicated than basic calls and puts to jaw-droppingly more so. While basic spread strategies have two legs, the more advanced strategies have three or four legs, with intersecting profit profiles that are often named after their wild, multi-winged appearance, such as condors and butterfly spreads. Suddenly the basic two-option spread strategy seems relatively tame.

Higher Brokerage Permission Required

Spreads require a higher level of permission from your broker than some of the basic strategies and even some of the other two-legged strategies. Certain options trades will expose your portfolio to significant loss, and your broker will want to know that you have some idea what you're doing when trading these complex strategies. You'll need to apply to your broker and be accepted to trade specific options setups.

Higher Commissions

Here's great news for your broker: If you're trading spreads, you're going to incur higher commissions. Every trade consists of at least two legs, so you're prone to racking up at least twice the commission on every single trade. Plus, some spreads have three or four legs, so the commissions can easily continue to grow if you're trading the more complex strategies. Of course, options commissions are typically priced on a per-contract basis, so the more contracts you move—even as part of the same trade—the more you'll pay. While you'll avoid incremental fees if you let your spreads expire, the nature of spreads—where you do need to actively take risk on and off—means that you shouldn't skimp here. You don't want the relatively cheap cost of a commission to lead to a bad decision that could cost you 100 times more.

Limited Returns

Spreads limit your returns, at least within certain bounds. That's the trade-off for limiting risk, which is a key advantage of spreads. Advanced traders appreciate the ability of spreads to limit risk to what they find attractive, and the limited returns may be more attractive given the risks.

Increased Risk Around Opening and Closing the Trade

The double, triple, or quadruple legs of spreads requires you to open and close your trades carefully. Typically, traders enter a basic spread by buying legs at the same time in a single trade, and it's safer than placing trades for multiple legs in separate trades. Sometimes your target stock may move quickly, leaving you with only one leg of the spread completed. More complex strategies may require you to open and close in multiple steps, leaving some real, albeit small, chance of the market moving unfavorably. This scenario could put you in a risky situation, especially if the stock continues to run unfavorably. You'll also need to take care as you unwind a multi-leg strategy, since you can end up with unwanted risks, such as an uncovered call. You can unwind a leg and suddenly have a lot more uncapped risk in your portfolio, so you'll need the margin capacity to handle it. If you suddenly have new unhedged risks, your broker will quickly reduce the amount you can safely borrow on margin.

Limited Risk, Limited Returns

The advantages of spread strategies are often directly tied to their disadvantages. Spreads limit risk, but the cost of this advantage is limited returns. They allow you to segment risk better, but they are more complex to set up and manage.

VERTICAL, HORIZONTAL, AND DIAGONAL SPREADS

Three Major Types of Spreads Explained

The nature of spread strategies is to offer a hedged trade with two or more legs, allowing you to segment risk to areas where you're finding attractively priced risk. Spread options strategies have three major types, depending on the dimension that is being spread for profit:

- **Vertical spread:** This spread uses options on the same underlying asset and same expiration but uses different strike prices to create the potential for profit.
- **Horizontal spread:** This spread (also called a calendar spread) uses options on the same underlying asset and strike price but uses different expirations to create the potential for profit.
- **Diagonal spread:** This spread mixes the attributes of the vertical and horizontal spreads, using options on the same underlying asset but adjusting the expirations and strike prices to create the potential for profit.

This section covers these types of spreads in more depth, offering some popular examples of each.

VERTICAL SPREADS

Vertical spreads use the same type of option (calls or puts), the same expirations on the paired options, but different strike prices, effectively isolating the price element in the trade. This setup means that the spread profits from a change in the price of the underlying asset, reducing the impact of implied volatility and time decay. This all means that the spread's profitability hinges on whether the underlying asset moves or not. Spread strategies limit risk as well as return, but despite the capped return profile, vertical spreads can still offer attractive returns if well structured. Vertical spreads with a net debit offer the ability to multiply the premium but only up to a point. In contrast, vertical spreads with a net credit offer an up-front payment and a capped downside. Vertical spreads include the following:

- **Bull call spread:** a low-strike long call with a high-strike short call for a net debit
- **Bear put spread:** a high-strike long put with a low-strike short put for a net debit
- **Bear call spread:** a high-strike long call with a low-strike short call for a net credit
- **Bull put spread:** a low-strike long put with a high-strike short put for a net credit

Each of these vertical spread types has its own pros and cons, just like the following horizontal spreads.

HORIZONTAL SPREADS

Horizontal (or calendar) spreads use the same type of option (calls or puts), the same strike price, but different expirations on the paired options, effectively isolating the time element in the trade. This isolation allows the trade to profit from relative changes in the volatility and time value of the two contracts, while capping the overall risk and return. A rise in implied volatility affects longer-term options more than shorter-term options, increasing the price of a long horizontal spread. For example, a long horizontal spread, which consists of a near-term short option and a later-dated long option, would increase in value if implied volatility rose. Horizontal spreads arbitrage the passage of time on two different expirations, since the time value of a short-term option erodes more quickly than that of a longer-term option. Horizontal spreads include the following:

- **Long calendar spread with calls:** a near-term short call paired with a longer-term long call for a net debit
- **Long calendar spread with puts:** a near-term short put paired with a longer-term long put for a net debit
- **Short calendar spread with calls:** a longer-term short call paired with a near-term long call for a net credit
- **Short calendar spread with puts:** a longer-term short put paired with a near-term long put for a net credit

The horizontal spreads can be combined with vertical spreads to create the next category: diagonal spreads.

DIAGONAL SPREADS

Diagonal spreads use the same type of option (calls or puts) but adjust both the expiration and strike prices of the contracts, forming a hybrid of the horizontal and vertical spreads. This setup allows the spread to profit on changes in implied volatility and the price of the underlying stock while still limiting risk along those same dimensions (i.e., for some period or some move in the stock price). Because of the mismatched expirations, diagonal spreads allow you to take risk on or off during the lifetime of the longer-dated option by adding a new paired option when the initial near-dated option expires. Similarly, the mismatched strike prices mean that you can pair a new contract to the existing long option at a more advantageous strike price. Diagonal spreads include the following:

- **Long diagonal spread with calls:** a low-strike, long-term long call paired with a high-strike, short-term short call for a net debit
- **Long diagonal spread with puts:** a high-strike, long-term long put paired with a low-strike, short-term short put for a net debit
- **Short diagonal spread with calls:** a low-strike, long-term short call paired with a high-strike, short-term long call for a net credit
- **Short diagonal spread with puts:** a high-strike, long-term short put paired with a low-strike, short-term long put for a net credit

Diagonal spreads can generate significant gains if used skillfully and can also produce recurring cash with a lower up-front investment than a covered call.

OTHER HYBRID OPTIONS STRATEGIES USING SPREADS

Spread strategies are popular with advanced traders because they allow you to fine-tune the risk you're taking while still offering attractive returns. So, traders have come up with a variety of other hybrid strategies that combine spreads with each other or with other basic options strategies, developing some wild names for them along the way. For example, butterfly spreads and condor spreads combine bull and bear vertical spreads into a new strategy that's beyond just the entry-level vertical spread. These strategies have variants, too, such as the iron butterfly or iron condor and the broken wing butterfly and broken wing condor. Then there's the Christmas tree spread, the albatross, the jelly roll, and the jade lizard, the latter of which combines a spread with a basic option. It's hard not to wonder where they come up with the striking names for these strategies. Some of the evidence is in the profit lines on an option's return profile.

While some of the more arcane strategies are beyond the scope of a 101 book, this text still runs through popular strategies such as butterfly spreads and condor spreads. These strategies offer plenty of complexity and opportunity to a new options trader.

The Benefit of Spread Strategies

Spread strategies offer significant opportunities for traders who have a well-defined view on how a stock will trade. They can be structured to create returns on stocks that are moving up and down, a little or a lot, or even just moving sideways.

BULL CALL SPREAD

Turbocharged Gains with Lower Risk

The bull call spread pairs two options—a long call and a short call—to create an attractive strategy that can work well with rising stocks, even those rising at moderate levels. In a bull call spread, you buy a low-strike call, often around the current stock price, and sell a higher-strike call. In this spread, both options are at the same expiration, making it a vertical spread. You expect the stock to finish at or above the higher strike price by expiration.

The potential upside on this strategy is the difference in the strike prices of the two options minus the cost of setting up the trade. If this trade is well structured, it could return up to a few times the setup cost if the stock rises even modestly, though the total return is capped. The downside is limited to the net debit on the trade. This spread is emblematic of buying and selling risk, with you buying the risk above the lower strike but then selling off any further gain above the higher strike.

WHEN TO USE THE BULL CALL SPREAD

The bull call spread is a useful strategy when the underlying stock is expected to rise, but it can be used even if the stock is just expected to make a medium gain. This trade's lower setup price—reduced by the sale of a higher-strike call—helps raise this strategy's percentage gains, but only up to the higher strike price. Between the two strike prices, however, this strategy generates higher returns than a long call alone. Because of this structure, this strategy doesn't need a soaring stock to work well, and a stock that can hit the higher strike will suffice to deliver this strategy's maximum returns. At any price above the high strike, the trade's profit maxes out. Despite the short call, this trade is safe even if the stock soars, as long as you own the long call.

Bullish on Bull Call Spreads

The bull call spread can be effective in situations where a stock is expected to rise but not soar. The spread's lower all-in cost allows you to multiply money without needing the stock to move as much as required by a long call strategy.

HOW TO MODIFY THE BULL CALL SPREAD

A key modification for the bull call spread is to adjust the strike prices to find an all-in cost that's attractive to you while balancing the potential upside of the trade. Strikes that are too close won't offer enough potential upside. At the same time, a high-price strike that's too far above the low-price strike won't offer enough premium to reduce the all-in cost even if it does offer the potential for more gain overall. So, it's important to figure out your potential return to see if it's worth the price. You may decide that a gain that's capped at two times the all-in cost may not be worth the potential loss of the investment. You may need more potential upside, and a greater spread between the strikes may offer more potential gain.

You can also adjust the expirations to give the stock more time to reach the upper strike and for the thesis to play out. But it's important to balance the costs and potential returns.

THE PROFIT POTENTIAL OF A BULL CALL SPREAD

The profit potential is limited to the difference in the strikes minus the net cost to set up the strategy. The max profit occurs when the stock reaches the high strike price, and if the stock rises beyond that, the short strike continues to lose money, but the position is fully hedged by the lower-priced long strike. Run through this example to see how it could play out.

Stock XYZ is trading for $45.50 per share, and you think the stock could rise based on research. You can set up a bull call spread with a long strike at $45 and a short strike at $47.50, both expiring in three months. The long call costs $2.20, while the short call pays $1.20, for a net debit of $1 for the strategy. Here's the profit at various stock prices at expiration.

The bull call spread

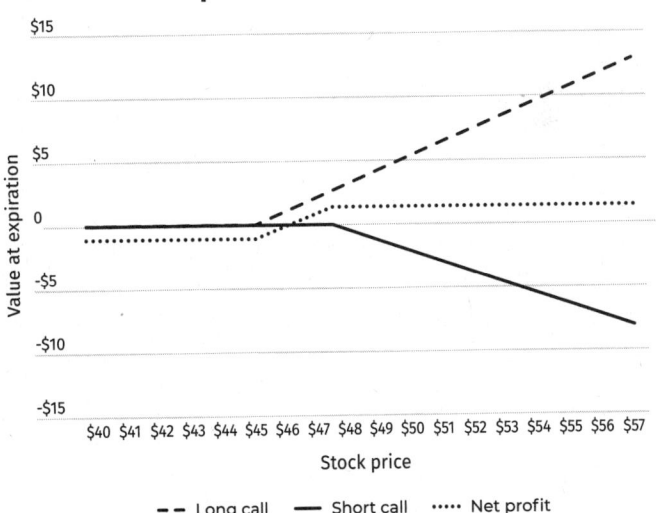

- The point of maximum profit occurs at the high strike price ($47.50) or above, where the option value flatlines at $2.50, as the short call's loss totally offsets the long call's gain.
- The trade breaks even at $46, or the $1 net cost plus the long strike price of $45. Between $45 and $46, the trade retains some value at expiration, though it's a net loser, with the short call expiring worthless at expiration.
- Below $45 at expiration, both calls expire worthless.

In this example, the strategy has a maximum value of $2.50, compared to a cost of $1, offering a potential 150% gain if the stock finishes expiration just 4.4% higher than today. If that return is not sufficient given the risk of the total loss of principal, you could set up a $45–$50 spread for a higher potential return.

WHAT TO WATCH FOR

It's important to pay attention to pricing dynamics, as the stock moves through strike prices. If the stock takes off in the early days or weeks of the trade, the spread's profit will increase but not as much as you might expect. For example, if the stock moved to $48 in two weeks, an options calculator suggests that the long call would be worth $3.65, while the short call would be worth $2.18, valuing the bull spread at $1.47. The short call moves up faster, percentage-wise, than the long call, as the stock moves through that strike price. As the stock moves up more, the strategy continues converging toward $2.50.

If the time value declines to little or nothing on an in-the-money short call, the call may be exercised. It's important to monitor this situation, since the exercise of the short calls could require significant cash or margin capacity in your account. To help avoid this situation, close out the position as the strategy approaches its max value.

If you want to close this strategy early, it's important to not leave the short calls unhedged. If you close a long call without closing a short call, you will need margin capacity to hold the unhedged call, and you expose yourself to extra risk if the stock rises. Close out the spread as a unit.

BEAR PUT SPREAD

Accelerated Profits on a Falling Stock

A bear put spread is much like a bull call spread, but it uses puts to profit when a stock falls. The bear put spread pairs a long put and a short put—to create a strategy that can return multiples of the net cost when a stock declines, even one that falls modestly. In a bear put spread you buy a high-strike option, typically around or somewhat below the current stock price, and sell a lower-strike put, with both options at the same expiration, creating a vertical spread.

The potential upside on this strategy is the difference in the strike prices of the two options minus the net cost of establishing the trade. If this trade is structured well, it could return a few times the all-in cost if the stock falls even moderately. The downside is limited to the net debit on the trade. Like the bull call spread, the bear put spread is a fine example of trading risk, as you buy the risk below the high strike and sell off any further gains below the low strike.

WHEN TO USE THE BEAR PUT SPREAD

The bear put spread can be a useful strategy when you expect the underlying stock to fall, and it can be used even if the stock is expected to fall only a moderate amount. The spread's lower setup cost—reduced by the sale of a put—raises this strategy's percentage gains, but only down to the lower strike price. Between the two strikes, this strategy generates higher percentage returns than a long put alone. With this structure, the strategy doesn't require a stock that can fall significantly to multiply the net investment, as would be the case with a long put only. Here, the stock needs to reach only the lower strike to max out the strategy's profit, and although the short strike loses money if the stock continues falling, the loss is fully hedged by the higher-priced long put. Despite the short put, this trade is safe even if the stock plummets, as long as you own the long put.

Losing Stock, Big Winner

The bear put spread can be a better strategy if you do not expect the stock to fall substantially. The spread's lower setup cost lets you potentially accelerate the investment gains without needing the stock to move as much as in a basic put strategy.

HOW TO MODIFY THE BEAR PUT SPREAD

A key modification for the bear put spread is to shift the strike prices to find an all-in cost that's attractive while balancing the potential upside of the trade. Strikes that are too near won't provide enough potential upside, while a low-price strike that's too far away won't offset the cost of the long put enough to significantly lower the trade's net cost, even if you do have more potential gain. You can figure out the maximum potential gain from the start to see if it's worth the cost and risk.

With a capped gain, you must determine whether a given trade's limited upside is worth the risk of losing the whole investment. You may decide you need more potential upside, and a greater spread between strikes may offer a more favorable wager. Setting up a longer-dated spread can also give the strategy more time to work.

THE PROFIT POTENTIAL
OF A BEAR PUT SPREAD

The bear put spread's profit potential is limited to the difference in the strikes less the net cost to set up the trade. The max profit occurs only if the stock finishes expiration at the low strike price or less. Run through the following example to see how it could play out.

Stock XYZ is trading for $50 per share, and you assume it could fall based on your research. You set up a bear put spread with a long strike at $50 and the short strike at $45, which is the next lowest, both expiring in three months. The long put costs $3.50, while the short put pays $1.70, resulting in a net debit of $1.80 for the trade. The following graph explores the profit at various stock prices at expiration.

Bear put spread

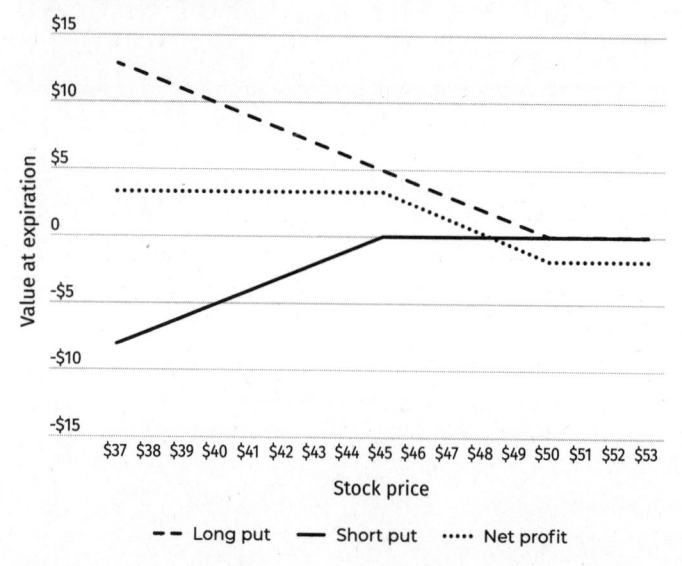

- The point of maximum profit occurs at the low strike price ($45) or below, where the strategy's value flatlines at $5, as the short put's loss totally offsets the long put's gain.
- The trade breaks even at $48.20, or the long strike price minus the $1.80 net cost. Between $48.20 and $50, the trade retains some value at expiration, with the short put expiring worthless at expiration, but it's a net loser overall.
- Above $45 at expiration, the short put expires worthless, while below $50, the long put is in the money and retains at least some value. Above $50 at expiration, both puts expire worthless.

In this example, the strategy has a maximum value of $5, compared to the all-in cost of $1.80, offering a potential 177.8% gain if the stock finishes expiration 10% lower than today. Given the significant move required, you must decide whether this potential gain is worth the risks.

WHAT TO WATCH FOR

It's vital to pay attention to pricing as the stock moves around the strike prices. If the stock moves in the early weeks of the trade, the spread's profit will increase but not as much as you might expect at first. As the stock falls even more, the strategy continues to converge toward the maximum difference of $5.

If the short put is deep in the money and time value declines to little or nothing, the put may be exercised before expiration. It's vital to keep an eye on this situation, since the exercise of the short puts could require significant cash or margin capacity in your account. To help avoid this situation, close out the position as the strategy approaches its maximum value.

If you want to close this strategy early, it's important to not leave the short puts unhedged. If you close a long put without closing a short put, you will need margin capacity to hold the unhedged put, and you expose yourself to extra risk if the stock falls. Close out the spread as a unit.

BEAR CALL SPREAD

Turn On Income from Calls with Less Risk

The bear call spread pairs two options—a short call and a long call—to create a strategy that works well with flat to declining stocks. In a bear call spread, you sell a lower-strike call and buy a higher-strike call at the same expiration, offering a net credit—income—for this vertical spread. Think of this strategy as an uncovered call that is de-risked with a higher-strike call as insurance to protect against the stock soaring.

The maximum potential upside to this strategy is the net credit when setting up the trade, and you keep the full credit if the stock is below the short strike at expiration. The maximum potential downside is limited to the differences in the two strike prices minus the net credit, in the case that the stock is above the long call at expiration. This strategy shows the nature of options as buying and selling risk, with strikes that create risk (short call) and reduce it (long call).

WHEN TO USE THE BEAR CALL SPREAD

The bear call spread is a useful strategy when the underlying stock is expected to fall, but it can be used even if the stock is expected to be flat until expiration. This strategy can be a better fit for stocks that are not expected to fall precipitously—though it can work there, too—but it offers only a limited cash payout rather than the chance to multiply the premium, which you could do with a more appropriate options strategy. With the bear call spread, the max profit occurs if the stock is below the short strike at expiration, so it can be helpful to pick a short strike that gives the stock a little room to move up but still be below the strike at expiration. The bear call spread can be used repeatedly to generate income with limited risk, and you could have a series of short-term spreads that are always expiring.

An Uncovered Call Re-Covered

The bear call spread removes some of the danger of writing an uncovered call, but it comes at the cost of buying insurance yourself against the stock making a bull move. This protection can make the otherwise risky uncovered short call more palatable.

HOW TO MODIFY THE BEAR CALL SPREAD

This spread can be modified in two important ways. First, you can adjust the difference between the strikes so that you generate enough return but don't take on too much risk. If the strikes are too close, your trade won't offer a lot of return, while too far apart and the setup may offer too much risk, even if it does pay better. So, carefully select a short strike that offers enough premium but is still likely to be above the stock price at expiration. Balance this issue with choosing a long strike that is not too costly yet doesn't offer the stock too much room to run up and raise the potential losses. Second, you can adjust where the strikes are relative to the stock price to increase or reduce your return. For example, if you're aggressive and want more cash and risk, you could lower the short strike below the current stock price. However, the stock must decline before expiration, or the short call will be exercised—a riskier setup than starting with the stock under the short strike. Check the trade's maximum return against the maximum downside to see the best and worst cases.

Of course, you can also adjust the expiration to generate a higher return, but match it to the period when you expect the stock to show weakness. A series of shorter spreads is likely to generate more income than a larger spread over the equivalent period.

THE PROFIT POTENTIAL OF A BEAR CALL SPREAD

The profit potential of a bear call spread is limited to the net credit received when you set up the strategy, and it only occurs if the stock finishes expiration at or below the short strike. The long call hedges the short call, so the strategy's loss tops out if the stock finishes expiration at or above the higher strike price. This strategy may often use strikes that differ by $5–$10 for stocks in the normal trading range. Here's an example.

Stock XYZ is trading for $29.50 per share, and you think it could fall soon as the market overall declines moderately. You set up a bear call spread with a short strike at $30 and a long strike at $35 for the next three months. The short call pays $2.25, while the long call costs $0.75, leaving a net credit of $1.50. Here's the profit on the trade.

Bear call spread

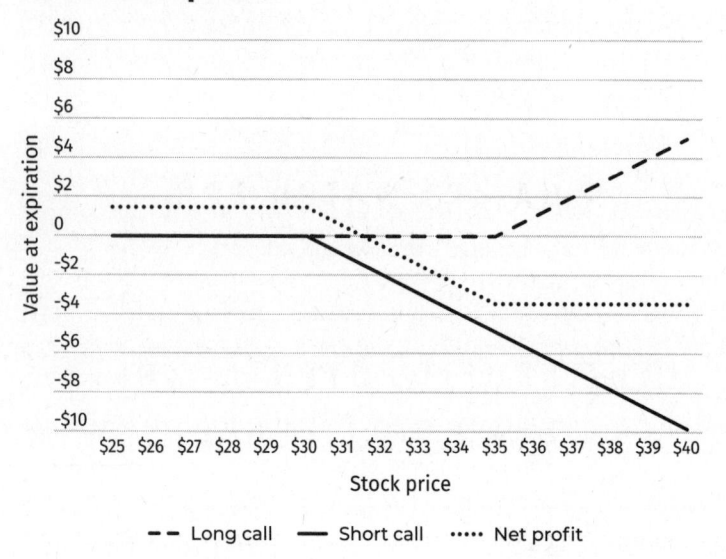

- The maximum profit occurs at or below $30, where the short call expires worthless. At any price under $35, the long call also expires worthless.
- The trade breaks even at $31.50, or the short strike plus the net premium. Between $30 and $31.50, the trade earns some profit but not all of it.
- Above $31.50, the trade begins to lose money, and it will continue to lose money until the stock reaches $35, at which point the protection of the long call begins. At any price above $35, the long call fully offsets any stock gain, at least at expiration. At $35 or above, you are left with the maximum possible loss of $3.50, or the $5 difference between the strikes offset by the net premium of $1.50.

This strategy offers a maximum profit of $1.50, compared to a maximum possible downside of $3.50. If the stock simply stays flat by expiration, you can claim the whole net premium, and of course, any further decline offers no more potential gain.

WHAT TO WATCH FOR

If the stock falls significantly and soon after the trade has been set up, it could make sense to close the trade, depending on whether the stock has any real chance of rebounding by expiration. But it's more likely that you'll end up holding open the trade and letting time continue to whittle away any remaining value. In this scenario, the long call will be all but worthless early.

It's important to remember that the long call is your protection in this strategy, and you don't want an uncovered call hanging out there if it has any chance of going in the money. In general, don't close out the long call unless you're also closing out the short call. Remember, you can do it as a single trade.

If the stock runs up way above the short strike or the short call is in the money and has little time value remaining, the call may be exercised. Keep a close eye as expiration approaches, and consider closing the trade as time value peters out and exposes an in-the-money short call to a potential exercise.

BULL PUT SPREAD

Turn a Stock's Rise Into Income

The bull put spread works much like a bear call spread but uses puts to wager on a stock rising or staying flat. In a bull put spread, you sell a higher-strike put and buy a lower-strike put at the same expiration, offering a net credit for this vertical spread. This strategy functions like a short put that you're de-risking by buying a long put at a lower strike as insurance that the stock doesn't plummet.

The maximum potential upside to this strategy is the net credit that is paid up front, and you retain the full credit if the stock finishes expiration above the short strike. The maximum loss is limited to the difference in the two strike prices less the net credit, which occurs if the stock is below the long put at expiration. This spread shows how you can use options to exchange and limit risk.

WHEN TO USE THE BULL PUT SPREAD

The bull put spread is appropriate if the underlying stock is anticipated to rise, but it can also be used if the stock is expected to trend sideways until expiration. This strategy can be a better fit for stocks that are not expected to soar, though it can work there, too, as this spread offers only a limited cash payout rather than the opportunity to multiply the premium offered by a long call. Here the max profit occurs if the stock remains above the short strike at expiration, so it can be useful to select a short strike that gives the stock some room to fall but still stay above the strike at expiration. The bull put spread can be used repeatedly to generate regular income on stocks that are rising, so you may have a series of these spreads that are always ticking down to profit.

Protect Your Downside

A short put by itself can show a substantial loss if the stock plummets. But tacking on a strategically placed long put to create a bull put spread keeps you from being totally exposed to the stock's potential fall, making a risky strategy more attractive.

HOW TO MODIFY THE BULL PUT SPREAD

You can modify this strategy in two significant ways: by adjusting the difference between the strikes to balance the risk and return, and by positioning the strikes relative to the stock price. If the strikes are too near, the trade won't offer enough return, but if they're too far apart, the strategy may offer too much risk, despite a larger payout. So, it's key to select a short strike that offers enough premium and to balance it with a long strike that doesn't raise potential downside too much. This strategy may use strikes that differ by $5–$10 for stocks in the typical trading range. Second, you can adjust the strikes relative to the stock price to raise or lower your up-front payout. The trade might be typically set up with the stock somewhat above the short put, so the stock can stay flat, rise, or maybe even decline just a little bit and the trade can still earn the full net premium. If you're more aggressive, you can set it up with the stock between the strikes, offering more return and more risk. Here the stock must rise above the short strike before expiration for you to receive the full net credit. Check the trade's potential return against the potential downside to see the best and worst cases.

THE PROFIT POTENTIAL OF A BULL PUT SPREAD

The profit potential of a bull put spread is capped at the net credit received when the trade is set up, and you get it only if the stock finishes expiration at or above the short strike. The long put hedges the short put, capping this strategy's risk, and the maximum loss tops out if the stock finishes expiration at or below the lower strike price. Review this example to see how it plays out.

Stock XYZ is trading for $30 per share, and you think it could rise soon as the market trends up. Set up a bull put spread to play this moderate rise using a short strike at $30 and a long strike at $25 for the next three months. The short put pays $2.75, while the long put costs $1, providing a net credit of $1.75 for setting up the spread. Here's the profit at various stock prices at expiration.

Bull put spread

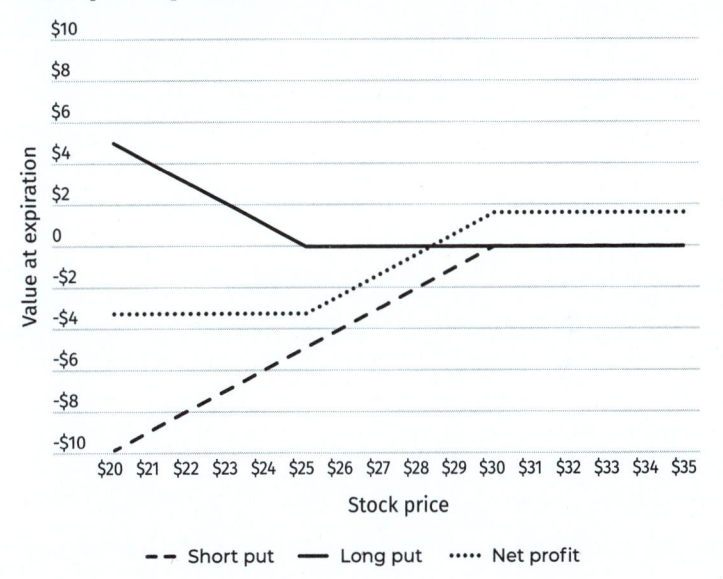

- The maximum profit occurs at or above $30, where the short put expires worthless. At any price above $25, the long put also expires worthless.
- The trade breaks even at $28.25, or the short strike minus the net premium. Between $28.25 and $30, the trade earns some profit.
- Below $28.25, the trade starts to lose money, and it will keep losing money until the stock hits $25, when the protection from the long put begins. At any price below $25, the long put completely offsets the stock's fall, at least at expiration. At $25 or below, you're left with the maximum potential loss of $3.25, or the $5 difference between the strikes reduced by the net credit of $1.75.

With this bull put spread, you keep the full payout if the stock stays flat or moves up. A more aggressive setup with the short strike above the current stock price—say, at $32.50—requires the stock to actively move up for you to keep the entire net premium.

WHAT TO WATCH FOR

If the stock rises substantially and soon after the trade has been set up, it could make sense to close the trade, assuming the stock has a real chance to fall again by expiration. However, a better move may be to hold open the trade while the passage of time continues to reduce any remaining value. In this case, the long put would be virtually worthless early on.

As in the bear call spread, the long option here is your protection against a bad loss, and you don't need an unhedged short put out there that could quickly become valuable. It's important not to close out the long put unless you're also closing out the short put first, and you can exit the trade as a unit.

If the stock plunges way below the short put or time value declines to little on an in-the-money short put, the put may be exercised, and you'll be forced to buy the stock. Consider closing the trade as time value approaches zero and exposes an in-the-money short put to a potential exercise.

LONG CALENDAR SPREAD WITH CALLS

Turning Time Into Money with Calendar Spreads

The long calendar spread with calls uses two call options to create a hedged position that can deliver low-risk but usually limited returns. In this calendar spread, you sell a near-term call and buy a far-term call at the same strike for a net debit, typically with the stock at or above the strike and for a short duration. For example, you might sell the front month's call and buy the subsequent month's call.

This strategy delivers the highest return at the first expiration when the stock is at the strike price. If this trade is set up well, the short-term call expires worthless, and you still have a long call that could rise uncapped. This spread profits on the faster time decay in the last weeks of the short call's life, while using the long call to hedge the short call against a spike in the stock. If the short call expires worthless, you must quickly decide what to do with the long call: sell or hold. The downside is limited to the net debit.

WHEN TO USE THE LONG CALENDAR SPREAD WITH CALLS

This long calendar spread can be an attractive strategy for stocks that stay near the strike during the life of the short call. The spread is frequently used in short-term setups, often with expirations of one to three months, and you can "harvest" a call's last few weeks of time value and then set up another spread and do it again. The spread takes advantage of the decay in the option's value, a decline that accelerates as the option approaches expiration. While the spread profits on a stock that finishes below the short strike price, it's not advantageous for the stock to fall much either, since a substantial decline hurts the value of the long call and could swing the trade to a loss.

A long calendar spread can also take advantage of how near-term calls and longer-term calls respond differently to changes in implied volatility. If implied volatility rises, it can make the longer-term call relatively more valuable. So, it may be advantageous to set up this spread when the implied volatility on the options is low but could move higher, boosting what an eventually unhedged long call could be sold for.

Act Fast on These Spreads

If the short call expires worthless, you are left with a long call and often just a month or two until expiration. Like the short call that preceded it, the long call will quickly lose value, so you must decide soon whether the call has more upside.

HOW TO MODIFY THE LONG CALENDAR SPREAD WITH CALLS

A primary way to adjust this spread is by changing the strike price relative to the stock price. For the strike, you'll want to find a price that's near where you expect the stock to be at expiration and balance that against the chances of the short strike expiring in the money over the duration of the call. You'll get a lot of premium if the strike is at the money or just above it, but you expose the short call to more risk of being in the money at expiration. This spread can also be set up on a short timeline, letting you capture the fast-declining time value quickly and then setting up the trade again and again. Harvesting a series of near-term calls can be more lucrative than the equivalent time in a single longer call.

THE PROFIT POTENTIAL OF A LONG CALENDAR SPREAD WITH CALLS

The profit potential is capped at specific periods in the life of this spread. Until the short call expires, the max profit is capped at the strike price. At this strike price, the strategy earns the full premium and the long call is at its highest value without sending the short call into the money. Above the strike price, the long call rises and offsets some of the increasing loss on the short call, as measured at the short call's expiration. If the short call expires worthless, the long call may have only weeks of life left, and you should carefully but quickly decide whether it makes sense to sell for the remaining value or hold for a potential gain. A surging stock or rising implied volatility could increase the value of this now-unhedged long call.

For example, let's say stock XYZ is trading for $85.50 per share, and you think it could rise later, but that it will be flat for the near future. You set up a long calendar spread with calls at a strike of $85, with a short call expiring in one month and a long call expiring in two months. The short call pays $2.85, while the long call costs $3.75, leaving a net debit of $0.90 for the strategy. Here's the profit on this strategy at the first expiration.

Long calendar spread with calls

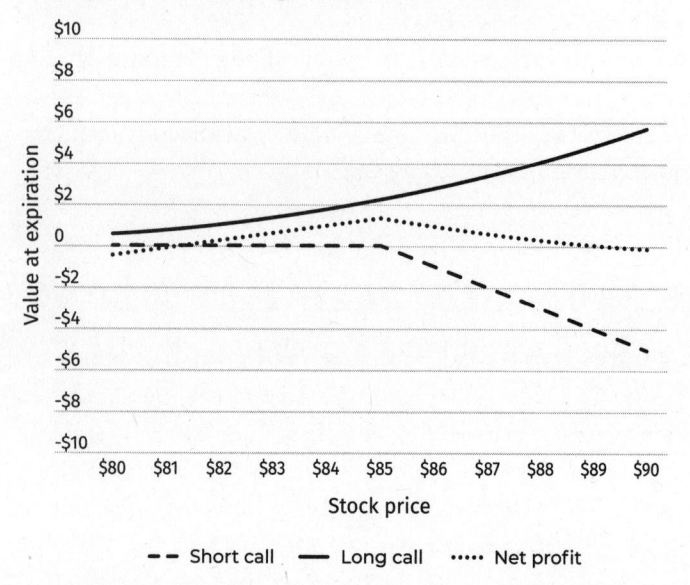

- Until the short call expires, the point of maximum profit occurs at $85, where the short call expires worthless and the long call increases in value. If the stock closes at $85 on the short call's expiration, the long call would be worth about $2.21, according to an options calculator. So, you now own a long call that was purchased for a net $0.90. If the short call expires worthless, the unhedged long call can keep rising for its remaining life.
- If the stock falls substantially, the long call may also expire worthless later at its expiration. The maximum downside here is the net cost of the trade, or $0.90 at the start.

WHAT TO WATCH FOR

The long calendar spread takes advantage of the difference in time decay, namely its acceleration, as the option approaches expiration as well as any differences in how the calls respond to volatility. If the short call expires and the stock is below the strike price, the now-unhedged long call may have little time to go in the money. Holding the call may make sense if you think the stock is set to move higher soon, but it's important to understand that time value is melting every day. So, anticipate your next action.

If the stock runs too high above the strike and time value declines to little on the in-the-money short call, the call may be exercised. The exercise could require significant cash or margin capacity.

Using the same principles, a long calendar spread with puts—buying a long-term put and selling a short-term put at the same strike price—offers a similar payoff.

LONG DIAGONAL SPREAD WITH CALLS

Generate Cash Now and a Large Gain Later

The long diagonal spread with calls uses two call options to create a hedged position that can deliver moderate to strong returns depending on how it's set up. In this diagonal spread, you buy a long-term call at a lower strike and sell a near-term call at a higher strike price for a net debit. You expect the stock to stay below the short-term strike at its expiration but rise well above the long-term strike at its later expiration, resulting in a potentially strong long-term gain.

The potential upside on this strategy is initially capped by the short-term call, but the long-term call can give this strategy significant upside over time. If this trade is set up well, the short-term call expires worthless, and you still hold a longer-term call with uncapped upside. The downside is limited to the net debit on the trade. The hedged nature of this trade—where the long call offsets the risk of the short call—reduces the loss potential of the short call.

WHEN TO USE THE LONG DIAGONAL SPREAD WITH CALLS

This diagonal spread can be an attractive strategy for stocks that stay flat or rise modestly in the short term but that can rise a lot over the duration of the long call. Initially, the max profit is capped at the short strike until it expires. If the stock exceeds the short strike, the long call hedges that loss fully, at least at expiration. If the short call expires worthless, the long call remains and offers further uncapped profit. Then, this trade can be set up again with another short call and the existing long call. Even if the stock rises, you can continue to sell calls with the protection of the long call as a hedge. By using LEAPS options as the long calls, you can rewrite short calls over and over, giving the bull thesis time to play out.

This strategy functions much like a covered call, but you're selling calls against your long call rather than a stock, earning this spread the nickname "the poor man's covered call." It's a much more efficient way to generate the income from a hedged short call, rather than being invested in the stock, which requires more capital. So, you could buy a $100 stock and write options on it or a $10 call and do the same.

A Strong Long-Term Options Play

If the short call of this diagonal spread expires worthless, you're left with a long-term call that may rise many times in value before it expires. This situation gives you choices: set up a new short call, sell the long call, hold on for more gains, or something else entirely.

HOW TO MODIFY THE LONG DIAGONAL SPREAD WITH CALLS

This spread can be adjusted by changing the strike prices and expirations. For the long strike, a LEAPS call that's at the money or a little out of the money can offer good value and give your bullish thesis time to work. For the short strike, balance the premium against the chances of the call expiring in the money. You'll get more premium if the short strike is just out of the money, but you run more risk of being in the money at expiration. But if the short strike is higher, you get less premium and have a larger all-in cost. You can increase the premium on the short call by extending the expiration but at the risk of more time for the call to go in the money. This strategy offers many variables, letting you fine-tune it based on your expectations.

THE PROFIT POTENTIAL OF A LONG DIAGONAL SPREAD WITH CALLS

The profit potential is capped at specific periods in the life of this spread. Until the short call expires, the max profit is capped at the short call's strike. At this strike price, the strategy earns the full premium from the short call, and the long call is at its highest value without sending the short call into the money. Above this strike, the long call will rise and offset the increasing loss on the short call at expiration. If the short call expires worthless, the remaining long call may have weeks or many months of uncapped upside left. Here's an example.

Stock XYZ is trading for $83.50 per share, and you think it could rise based on your research, but that it may take time before the market recognizes its potential. You can set up a long diagonal spread with an $85 long call and a $90 short call, with the short call expiring in four months and the long call expiring in two years. The short call pays $2.40, while the long call costs $12.20, leaving a net debit of $9.80 for the strategy. Here's the profit on this strategy at the first expiration.

Long diagonal spread with calls

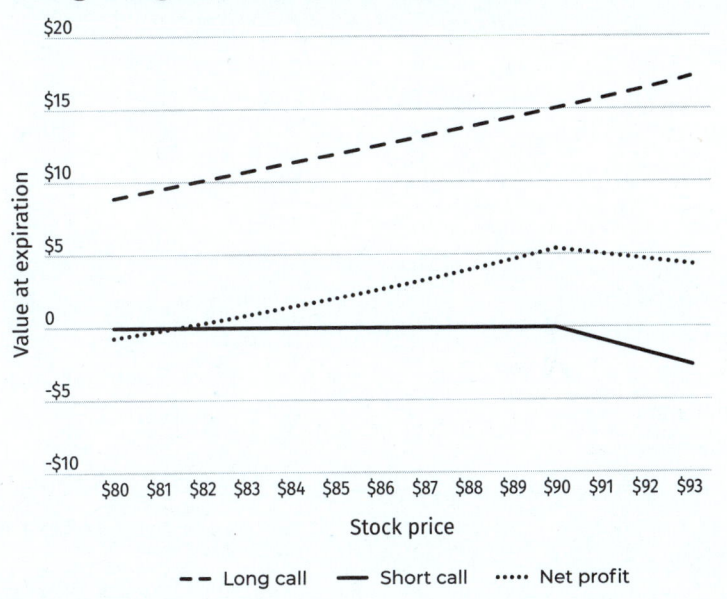

- Until the short call expires, the point of maximum profit occurs at $90, where the call begins to lose money and is offset some by the rising long call. If the stock closes at $90 on the short call's expiration, the long call would be worth about $14.80, according to an options calculator. If the short call expires worthless, the long call can rise for 20 further months.
- If the short call expires worthless, the trade breaks even at $94.80 at expiration, or the $85 strike plus the net cost of $9.80. In this case, you can sell another call, effectively lowering the net cost of the long call, and do so over and over.
- If the stock falls, stays flat, or even rises somewhat, the short call expires worthless. If the stock falls, the value of the long call is at

risk. The maximum downside here is the net cost of the trade, or $9.80 at the start.

WHAT TO WATCH FOR

The long diagonal spread can be a useful strategy if you have a long-term bullish outlook on the stock. When setting up the trade, adjust the strikes based on your expectation of how the stock will perform in the short and long term. As the stock rises over time, you can keep selling calls at even higher strikes against the protection of the long call and end up with a long call that may have multiplied in value over time.

If the stock runs too high above the short strike and little time value remains on the short call, the call may be exercised. The exercise could require significant cash or margin. Like other strategies with short calls, if you close this strategy, don't leave the short calls unhedged. You could also consider closing out the short calls at a loss and then setting up a new short call at a longer expiration at a higher strike price.

Using the same principles, a long diagonal spread with puts—buying a long-term, high-strike put and selling a short-term, lower-strike put at a near-term expiration—offers a similar payoff.

Chapter 7

More Multi-Leg Spread Options Strategies

This chapter covers even more advanced spread strategies and moves into the wilder three- and four-legged trades that continue to carve out risk and return for traders with a well-defined view of how a stock is likely to trade. More complex spreads tend to offer significant (and easier) chances to profit, but these often limit the potential upside further than the simpler spread strategies. To put it another way, to succeed you'll need to have a lot of little wins rather than just a few big wins.

One disadvantage of more complex spreads is the higher commissions, which could easily cost four times what a core options strategy takes to set up and even twice as much as a two-leg spread. Those commissions could hit you not only on the way in but also when you close out the spread, so it's important that you understand the higher frictional costs here. The costs of the bid-ask spread could also be significant, given the many different trades in these complex strategies. Since multi-leg spreads generate more limited profits, commissions and bid-ask costs may take a surprisingly large bite here.

LONG BUTTERFLY SPREAD WITH CALLS

Profit on a Stock Staying Flat

The long butterfly spread with calls is a three-legged strategy that profits from declining volatility and a relatively stable stock. In a long butterfly spread with calls, you buy a call at a low strike price, sell two calls at a higher strike, and buy one call at a still higher strike for a net debit. The calls have the same expiration, and the distance between all strikes is the same. This strategy is effectively a bull call spread (using the lower and middle strikes) and a bear call spread (using the middle and higher strikes), both of which share the same strike price in the trade's middle leg.

The maximum potential upside on this strategy is limited and occurs when the stock closes expiration at the middle strike; however, the stock could still return multiples of the net premium. Despite a high percentage upside, the total dollar gain on the butterfly spread is somewhat low. The downside is limited to the net debit on the trade. Because of the various legs, the broker's commission on this trade is going to be higher than it would be for a basic or spread strategy.

WHEN TO USE THE LONG BUTTERFLY SPREAD WITH CALLS

Because of its structure, the long butterfly spread offers limited risk and limited gain, and it can be a good strategy when you don't expect the underlying stock to move too much before expiration. You aim to have the stock finish expiration near the middle strike price, where its profit is greatest. The sale of the two middle strikes offsets the purchase of the higher and lower strikes, significantly reducing the all-in cost of the strategy, expanding its range of profitability. However, the stock has only a little room to fluctuate near that middle strike, higher or lower, before it starts to become a net loser overall. The strategy profits from lower volatility, so it can be useful to set up this strategy when implied volatility is currently high, such as before an earnings report, but could decline in the near future, such as after the report. If the stock moves significantly away from the middle strike, you lose the whole net premium.

Butterfly, Butterfly

This options strategy is named after the shape of the profit curve, with the lower and higher strikes forming the wings of the butterfly. The strategy's low net setup cost can help it deliver higher percentage gains, even if the total level of return in dollars is limited.

HOW TO MODIFY THE LONG BUTTERFLY SPREAD WITH CALLS

You can adjust the expirations on the strategy to provide a lower all-in cost. The long butterfly spread is often a short-duration strategy, but lengthening the expiration a bit can reduce the all-in cost and widen the range of profitability. With a longer expiration time, the middle short strikes at the money increase in value more than the low-strike, in-the-money long call, offsetting the all-in price more and expanding the breakeven zone. That greater probability of profit comes at the risk of more time for the stock price to fluctuate.

You can shift the spread so that the middle strikes are where you expect the stock to finish expiration. If you expect the stock to drift a bit lower by expiration, set up the middle strikes a bit lower, for example. If you're more aggressive, you may move the strikes much further away to increase potential returns but with much higher risk.

THE PROFIT POTENTIAL OF A LONG BUTTERFLY SPREAD WITH CALLS

The profit is limited to the difference between the middle strike and the low strike minus the net cost to set up the trade. That payoff occurs exactly at the middle strike, and it doesn't happen often, so you should expect a more modest return as the stock approaches expiration—that is, you're more likely near the bullseye rather than right in it. Here's an example to see how it works.

Stock XYZ is trading for $50, and you think it's going to stay flat over the coming month. You set up a long butterfly spread with calls expiring in a month, using strikes at $45, $50, and $55. The long calls (at $45 and $55) cost $5.50 and $0.35, and the two short calls (at $45) pay $1.80 each, for a net setup cost of $2.05. The graph shows the profit at various stock prices at expiration.

Long butterfly spread with calls

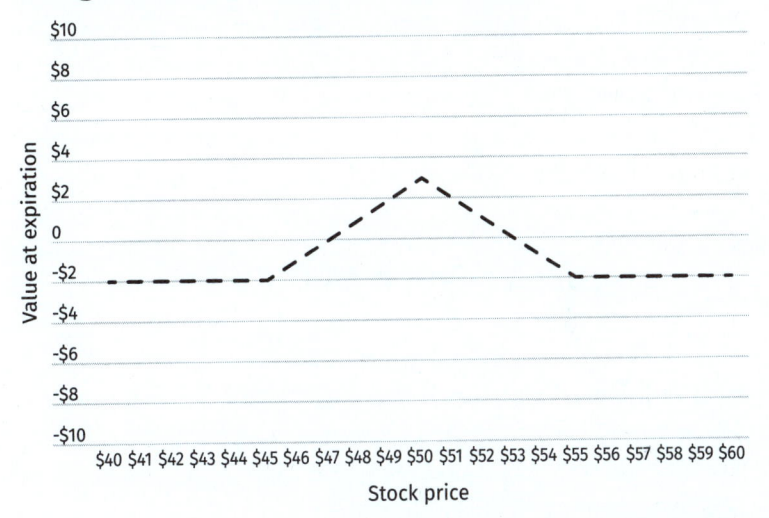

Value at expiration vs. Stock price

Net profit

- The maximum profit occurs at the middle strike ($50), where the middle strikes and high strike expire worthless, and the low strike is worth $5. Subtract the net debit of $2.05, and you'd earn $2.95 at this stock price.
- The trade breaks even at two places: $47.05 and $52.95, or the low strike plus the net debit and the high strike minus the net debit. In between that price range the trade makes some profit. Between $45 and $47.05, you'll still walk away with a little money, though you've lost money overall, and it's the same case between $52.95 and $55.
- Below $45 and above $55, you lose the entire net debit and walk away with nothing. Below $45, all options expire worthless, while above $55, the short and long calls exactly offset each other, leaving no profit.

This strategy has a maximum possible gain of $2.95 against an all-in cost of $2.05, but the likelihood of maxing out the gain here is virtually nonexistent. Instead, you should aim to be close to the place of maximum profit, ultimately settling for a much smaller total return. Given the low-risk, low-return nature of the strategy, you may need to put on many butterflies to earn a significant return in terms of total dollars, even if the percentage gain is adequate overall.

WHAT TO WATCH FOR

Because of options pricing dynamics, the prices on the legs of a butterfly spread may fluctuate a lot if the stock's volatility remains high. The expected convergence in the spread may require you to wait until the last few days of expiration, as the range of possible prices quickly narrows.

The short calls are integral to the spread, even in the last days of the trade, when pricing on the strategy may not have settled down. If the short calls are in the money and their time value declines to little, the calls may be exercised, derailing this strategy.

Perhaps unexpectedly, this strategy looks much like the long butterfly spread with puts. Both strategies profit the most when a stock stays within a narrow range in the middle of the trade rather than making a move in one direction or the other. Both strategies can be set up to play the same stock in each situation, and so the returns will look similar.

SHORT BUTTERFLY SPREAD WITH CALLS

Generate Cash with Higher Probability

The short butterfly spread with calls looks like the inverse of the similar long spread, but it profits from increasing volatility. In a short butterfly spread with calls, you sell a call at a low strike price, buy two calls at a higher strike, and sell one call at a still higher price for a net credit. The calls have the same expiration, and the distance between the strikes is the same. This strategy uses a bear call spread (at the lower and middle strikes) and a bull call spread (at the middle and higher strikes), both of which share the same strike price in the spread's middle leg.

The maximum potential upside on this strategy is limited to the net credit received, and it occurs when the stock closes expiration either below the lower strike or above the higher strike. The downside is limited, though you could lose multiples of the net credit if the stock finishes expiration right at the middle strike. Like other butterfly spreads, the multiple legs here create a more expensive trade to set up and close than a basic option or even a basic spread trade.

WHEN TO USE THE SHORT BUTTERFLY SPREAD WITH CALLS

The short butterfly spread with calls offers limited risk but limited gain, and it can be a useful strategy when you anticipate the underlying asset to move away from the middle strike before expiration. But it doesn't need to move far for the strategy to capture all the limited upside. The sale of the low and high strikes more than offset the two long calls at the middle strike, resulting in a net credit to set up the trade. If the stock moves beyond either the low or high strikes, the spread will capture the full premium. However, if the stock is anywhere near the middle strike at expiration, it can turn this trade into a net loser.

HOW TO MODIFY THE SHORT BUTTERFLY SPREAD WITH CALLS

You can adjust the expirations on the strategy to provide a higher or lower net credit, but the short butterfly spread works well as a short-duration strategy and can offer a higher net credit that way. A higher net credit provides a greater margin of safety and offers a wider window of stock prices where this trade earns at least some of that premium, though it will still only earn the full premium below the low strike and above the high strike. The benefit of this higher premium must be balanced against setting up a longer-duration but lower-paying trade that gives the stock more time to move away from the middle strike and earn the full premium. However, setting up a short butterfly with more days to expiration decreases the net credit and narrows the breakeven zone.

THE PROFIT POTENTIAL OF A SHORT BUTTERFLY SPREAD WITH CALLS

The profit is limited to the net credit when setting up the trade: the premium received from the high and low strikes offset by the cost of the two middle strikes. The max profit occurs when the stock finishes expiration below the low strike or above the high strike. You can still earn some of the premium, however, if the stock does not move too close to the middle strike. Here's an example.

Stock XYZ is trading for $70, and you think it's going to move either higher or lower over the coming month. You set up a short butterfly spread with calls expiring in a month, using strikes at $65, $70, and $75. The short calls (at $65 and $75) pay $5.30 and $0.20, and the two long calls (at $70) cost $1.60 each, for a net credit of $2.30.

Short butterfly spread with calls

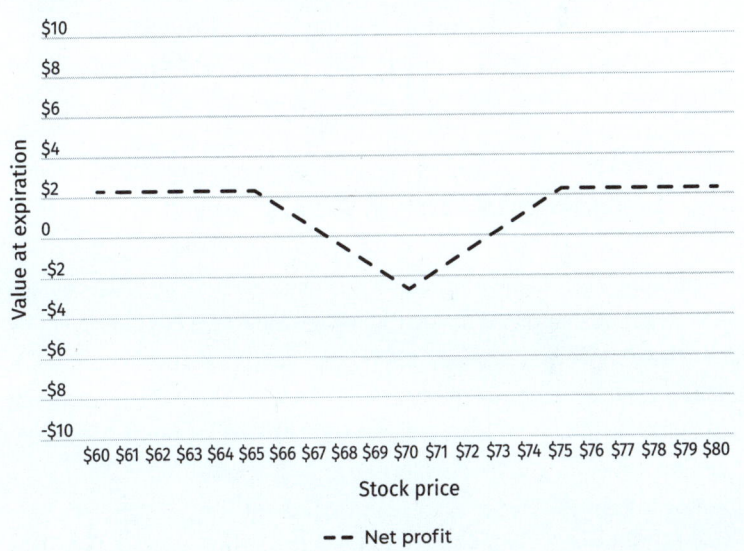

- - Net profit

- The maximum profit occurs beyond the low strike ($65) and the high strike ($75), where the strategy captures the full net premium of $2.30. The max loss occurs at the middle strike ($70), where the trade is valued at $5, resulting in a net loss of $2.70, or $5 minus the net credit.

- The trade breaks even at two places: $67.30 and $72.70, or the low strike plus the net credit and the high strike minus the net credit. In between those prices, the short spread results in a net loss.
- Between $65 and $67.30, you capture part of the net premium, and it's the same situation between $72.70 and $75. A higher net credit expands the breakeven zone.

This strategy has a maximum possible gain of $2.30 against a possible loss of $2.70, and you have a high probability of the setup keeping some, if not all, of the net credit. For the trade to lose money, the stock must finish between the narrow range of $67.30 and $72.70. It's a low-risk, low-return strategy that requires repeated success (or a really big wager) to really drive substantial profits.

WHAT TO WATCH FOR

You should pay particular attention to costs, given the number of legs here. The entry and exit may entail up to eight separate transactions per iteration of this strategy plus the potential costs of the bid-ask spread for each of those transactions. These frictional costs can eat up a larger-than-expected chunk of what is a limited-return strategy.

The strategy's two short calls—one of which is usually in the money to start the trade—could be exercised at any point, but it's only likely if they're in the money and have little time value remaining. So, it's important to pay careful attention to the potential exercise of the short calls, since it could eat up serious margin and foul up the trade near the end. If the stock is well below the low strike price, no options are likely to expire in the money, making this concern moot.

LONG IRON BUTTERFLY SPREAD

High-Probability Gains from Small Stock Moves

The long iron butterfly spread is a four-legged strategy that profits from rising volatility and a stock that is on the move. In this strategy, you sell a put at a low strike price and buy a put at a middle strike price, while also buying a call at the same middle strike and selling a call at a higher strike. The options have the same expiration, and the distance between the strikes is the same. This strategy is the same as a bear put spread and a bull call spread that share the middle strike price.

The maximum upside on the long iron butterfly is capped and occurs when the stock is below the low strike or above the high strike at expiration. The potential return is quite limited, but the strategy may work satisfactorily if the stock shows volatility. The downside is limited to the net debit, but the strategy can be expensive to set up, relative to the total return. Given the various legs, the commission and bid-ask costs will be higher than for a basic or spread strategy.

WHEN TO USE THE LONG IRON BUTTERFLY SPREAD

Its structure makes the long iron butterfly spread a limited-risk, limited-reward strategy, and it can be useful when you expect the stock to make an extreme move before expiration, beyond either the low or high strike. The purchase of the two middle strikes (a call and put) more than offsets the cash received from selling the low (put) and high (call) strikes, resulting in a net debit. The stock must make a move beyond the breakeven prices—the middle strike plus or minus the net debit—for the strategy to become profitable. If the stock simply sits near the middle strikes, or even inside the two breakeven points, the strategy expires worthless. So, it can be useful if the underlying stock ends up more volatile than expected at the start. A stock that's stable or may show declining volatility near the strategy's expiration is to be avoided.

HOW TO MODIFY THE LONG IRON BUTTERFLY SPREAD

You can adjust the expiration to offer a lower all-in cost, reducing the net debit. A shorter duration can reduce the cost to set up this trade, delivering a potentially higher total percentage return. This smaller net debit narrows the range of the breakeven prices, giving the trade even more room to earn at least some profit. But the advantage of a higher-probability win must be balanced with the reduced time available for the option to make a more extreme move past the high or low strikes, where profit is maxed out.

THE PROFIT POTENTIAL OF A LONG IRON BUTTERFLY SPREAD

The profit is limited to the difference between the low and middle strikes minus the net debit to set up the trade. This payoff occurs below the low strike and above the high strike. Here's an example to see how it works.

Stock XYZ is trading for $50, and you think it's going to move somewhat in the next two months. Suppose you set up a long iron butterfly spread expiring in two months, using strikes at $45, $50, and $55. The long call costs $1.65 and the short call pays $0.25, while the long put costs $1.30 and the short put pays $0.10. It all nets out to a debit of $2.60 to establish the trade. Here's the profit at various stock prices at expiration.

Long iron butterfly spread

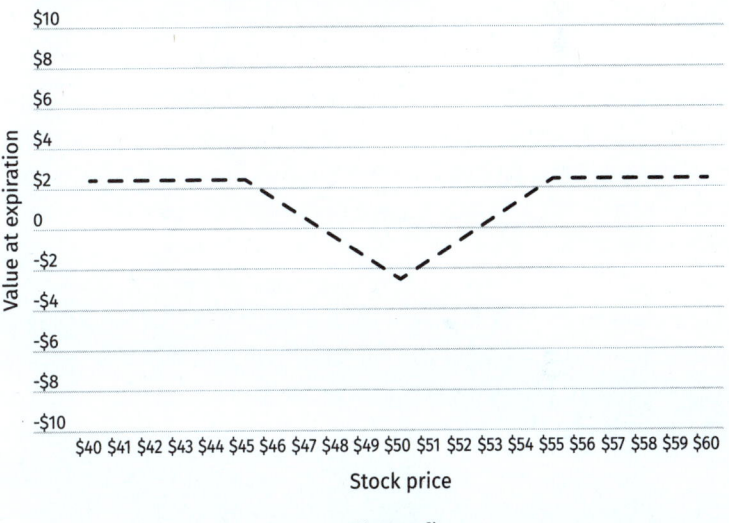

- The maximum profit occurs at any price below $45 or above $55, where either the bear put spread or bull call spread is worth its maximum value of $5. In other words, the stock is either beyond the low strike in the put spread or beyond the high strike in the call spread.

- The trade breaks even at two places: $47.40 and $52.60, or the middle strike plus and minus the cost of the net debit ($2.60). In between those breakevens, the trade expires totally worthless. Between $45 and $47.40, the trade makes some profit, as it does between $52.60 and $55.

This strategy has a maximum possible gain of $2.40 against an all-in cost of $2.60, but the price range where this trade loses—between just $47.40 and $52.60—gives it a higher probability of success. The stock needs to move about 5% in either direction over two months for this strategy to break even. However, the limited maximum return may be less attractive, given the risk of losing the whole net debit. The limited return means the strategy must be set up successfully many times or have a large bet to generate an attractive overall profit, even if it achieves its maximum profit each time.

WHAT TO WATCH FOR

The total value of an iron butterfly may fluctuate significantly if the stock is near the middle strike anywhere close to expiration and shows volatility. With a narrow range of total loss, the trade may quickly swing to a modest profit or even a full profit if the stock shows a small price change.

With the short call and short put in this spread, keep a close eye on those options if they're well in the money and have little time value remaining (i.e., if the stock is well beyond their strike prices). In this case, there's a risk of exercise, so if you've captured most of your profit here, it can make sense to close out the trade and eliminate the possibility of exercise.

The inverse strategy—the short iron butterfly—profits if the stock remains close to the middle strike and pays a net credit. Here you buy a put at a low strike price and sell a put at a middle strike, while also selling a call at the same middle strike and buying a call at a higher strike. It's the same as a bull put spread and a bear call spread that share the middle strike.

LONG CONDOR SPREAD WITH CALLS

A Low-Risk Wager on Low-Volatility Stocks

The long condor spread with calls is a low-risk, limited-return four-legged strategy that profits from low-volatility stocks. In a long condor spread, you buy a call at a low strike price, sell a call at a higher strike, sell another call at a still higher strike, and finally buy a call at yet another higher strike, all for a net debit. The calls have the same expiration, and the strikes are spaced equidistantly. The sale of the two middle strikes partially offsets the purchase of the lowest and highest calls, reducing the all-in cost. This strategy is a mix of a bull call spread (at the lower two strikes) and a bear call spread (at the higher two strikes).

The maximum upside on this strategy is limited and occurs when the stock closes expiration in between the two middle strikes. While the strategy could make a strong percentage return, the total gain here is somewhat limited. The downside is limited to the net debit, though costs will run up due to the multiple legs and bid-ask spreads when entering and exiting the trade.

WHEN TO USE THE LONG CONDOR SPREAD WITH CALLS

The long condor spread is structured to offer limited risk and limited gain, and it can be a useful strategy if you think the underlying stock won't move much before expiration. You want the stock to finish expiration between the middle strike prices, where its profit is greatest. This strategy is like the long butterfly spread with calls, which also aims for a stock to finish near the middle point of the strategy. In the long condor, however, the two middle strikes offer a wider range of stock prices to capture the max profit, increasing the chances of being right but at a reduced maximum profit potential, compared to the long butterfly. If the stock moves significantly higher or lower, or is likely to experience significant volatility, the whole net debit could be lost. The strategy profits from lower volatility, so it can be useful to start the trade when implied volatility is up but could decline in the near future, such as following an earnings report.

Condor versus Butterfly

The long condor spread is much like the long butterfly spread, and both profit most when the underlying stock stays near the middle of the setup. However, the long condor's setup allows you to maximize profits at more potential stock prices than the long butterfly spread does.

HOW TO MODIFY THE LONG CONDOR SPREAD WITH CALLS

You can shift the expirations on the strategy to lower the all-in cost. The long condor can work well over shorter durations, although extending the expiration can reduce the net debit and widen the range of profitability. With a longer expiration time, the middle short strikes at the money increase in value more than the low-strike long call, offsetting the all-in cost more and widening the breakeven zone. The flip side is that more time also gives the stock price more opportunity to fluctuate outside this profitable range.

You can also shift the middle strikes so that they "catch" the stock price when they reach expiration. If you expect the stock to drift higher by expiration, set up the middle strikes somewhat higher, for example.

THE PROFIT POTENTIAL OF A LONG CONDOR SPREAD WITH CALLS

The profit on this strategy is limited to the difference between the lower long call and the lower short call minus the net debit to set up the trade. The max payoff occurs anywhere between the two middle strikes, securing the best profit here on a wider variety of stock prices than a long butterfly, though the max total return is more modest because of that structure. Here's an example to see how it works.

Stock XYZ is trading for $52.50, and you think it's going to stay flat over the coming month. The graph provided here shows a setup of a long condor spread with calls expiring in a month, using strikes at $45, $50, $55, and $60. The calls are priced at $7.80, $3.65, $1.20, and $0.25, respectively, for a net setup cost of $3.20. Here's the profit at various stock prices at expiration.

Long condor spread with calls

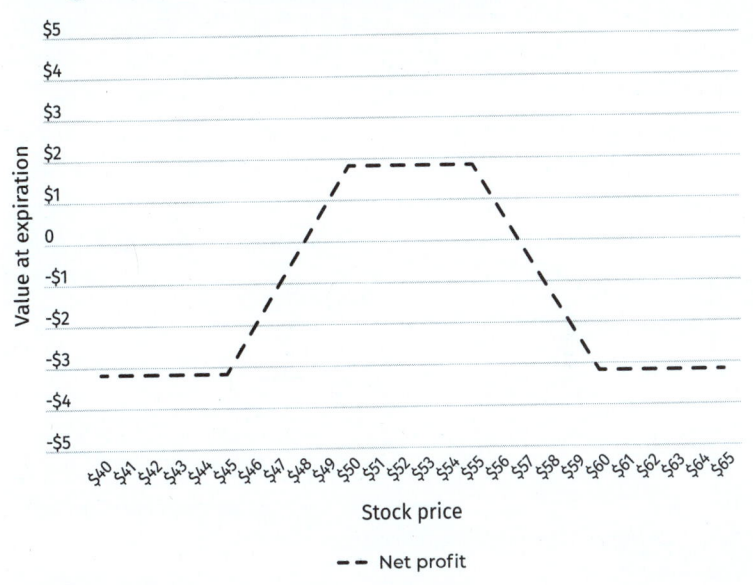

Stock price

-- Net profit

- The maximum profit occurs between the two middle strikes ($50 and $55), where the $55 and $60 calls expire worthless. At a stock price of $50–$55, the $45 long call is in the money, and the $50 short call fully offsets any marginal gain from the $45 long call, leaving this option pair worth $5. Subtract the net debit of $3.20, and you earn $1.80.
- The trade breaks even in two places: $48.20 and $56.80, or the low strike plus the net debit and the high strike minus the net debit. In between that range the trade makes some profit. Between $45 and $48.20, you'll walk away with some money, but the trade is a net loser, as is the case between $56.80 and $60.
- Below $45 and above $60, you lose the whole net debit. Below $45, all options expire worthless, while above $60, the two call spreads offset each other completely at expiration, leaving no profit.

The potential gain of $1.80 against the all-in cost of $3.20 may not be an attractive trade, depending on what you expect to happen. But the strategy does offer a wider range of stock prices to capture the maximum profit ($50–$55), compared to the long butterfly spread with calls. And the trade can turn at least some profit anywhere between $48.20 and $56.80, meaning the stock can move up or down about 8% and this trade will still be a net winner. A lower net debit would allow this trade to break even over an even wider range of prices.

WHAT TO WATCH FOR

The limited potential upside here means that you need to set up this trade successfully many times to earn a worthwhile return in total dollars, even if the percentage gain is adequate, or otherwise have a large wager on it.

Don't confuse the long condor spread with the long iron condor spread. The latter uses both puts and calls, setting up a bear put spread on the lower end of the condor and a bull call spread on the higher end, all at the same expiration and with equidistant strike prices. In contrast to the long condor, the long iron condor profits if the stock makes an extreme move higher or lower.

SHORT CONDOR SPREAD WITH CALLS

Income from Higher-Volatility Stocks

The short condor spread with calls is a four-legged strategy that is the inverse of the similarly named long condor spread. In the short condor with calls, you sell a call at a low strike price, buy a call at a higher strike, buy another call at a still higher strike, and finally sell a call at yet another higher strike, receiving a net credit. The calls have the same expiration, and the strikes are evenly spaced. The sale of the highest and lowest calls offsets the purchase of the two middle calls, offering a net credit to set up this strategy. The short condor is a mix of a bull call spread (at the higher two strikes) and a bear call spread (at the lower two strikes).

The maximum upside on this strategy is limited and is paid as a net credit when setting up the trade. You'll keep the full credit if the stock finishes expiration below the lowest strike or above the highest strike. The downside is limited to the difference between the strikes minus the credit. With so many legs, the condor may cost a lot in commissions and bid-ask spreads to set up and close.

WHEN TO USE THE SHORT CONDOR SPREAD WITH CALLS

The short condor spread with calls offers limited risk and limited gains, and it's a useful strategy if you think the stock will make a move from its current price before expiration. The short condor profits when the stock moves away from the middle strikes of the spread, either higher or lower. This strategy is like the short butterfly with calls, which also profits if the stock moves higher or lower. In the short condor, however, the two middle strikes offer a wider range of stock prices that can result in a trade being a net loser, raising the odds of this happening. This strategy is generally better when the stock shows volatility during the life of the options strategy, meaning that it may have a higher potential to exceed the extreme strikes at expiration and retain the full net credit.

HOW TO MODIFY THE SHORT CONDOR SPREAD WITH CALLS

You can decrease the expiration on the strategy to increase the net credit, though it's important to balance this consideration against the shorter period for the stock to move past the lowest and highest strikes. Less time to expiration means less ability for the stock to swing to full profitability or even to enter the zone where you keep some of the net credit. Conversely, more time to expiration offers a lower net credit but more potential for the stock to move significantly and capture the full premium beyond the extreme strikes.

THE PROFIT POTENTIAL OF A SHORT CONDOR SPREAD WITH CALLS

The max profit on the short condor is limited to the net credit when the trade is established, and you keep all of it if the stock closes expiration below the low strike or above the high strike. If the stock becomes less volatile and stays near the middle of the strategy, you may lose the whole net credit and be on the hook for even more money, up to the limited maximum loss here. Consider the following example to see how it works.

Stock XYZ is trading for $52.50, and you think it's going to move up or down over the coming month. You can set up a short condor spread with calls expiring in a month, using strikes at $45, $50, $55, and $60. The calls are priced at $7.80, $3.65, $1.20, and $0.25, respectively, for a net credit of $3.20. The graph provided here shows the profit at various stock prices at expiration.

Short condor spread with calls

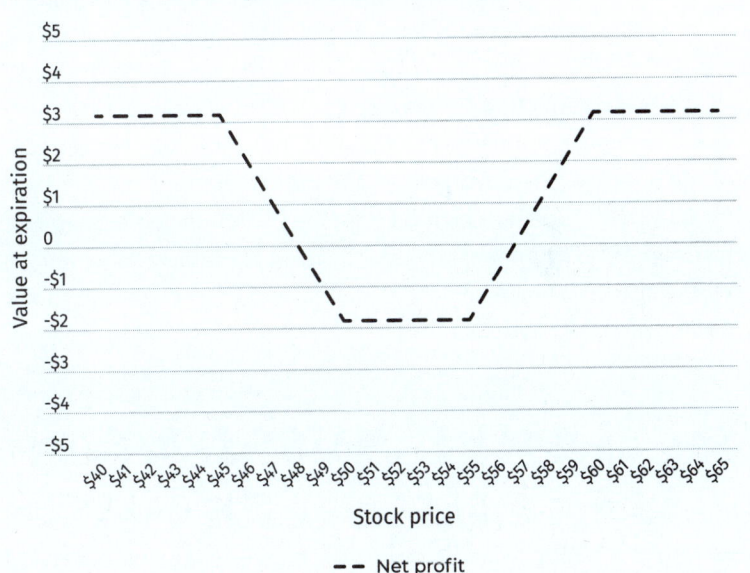

- The maximum profit occurs beyond the extreme strikes ($45 and $60). Below $45, all options expire worthless, while above $60, the two call spreads fully offset each other. In both scenarios you keep the whole net credit of $3.20.
- The trade breaks even in two places: $48.20 and $56.80, or the low strike plus the net credit and the high strike minus the net credit. Between $45 and $48.20, you'll keep some but not all the net credit, and the trade is still a net winner, as is the case between $56.80 and $60.
- Between $50 and $55, the trade loses a net $1.80. In this situation, the $60 short call and $55 long call expire worthless, while the $50 long call offsets the loss of the $45 short call only above $50, leaving this pair of options with a net value of –$5. Subtract the $3.20 credit for a net loss of $1.80.

The max gain of $3.20 against a max limited loss of $1.80 may seem attractive. But it's key to remember this strategy has a wider range of prices where you can suffer a total loss and a wide range where you may not get the full premium, compared to a similar butterfly spread. The limited potential upside means this trade needs to be executed successfully many times or have a large wager to earn a good total return in dollars.

WHAT TO WATCH FOR

For a stock that's poised to move, this strategy may be more favorable than the long straddle or long strangle, where you may need the stock to move much more for the trade to break even. While the maximum upside is limited on the short condor and not nearly as great as on those two strategies, it can be easier to realize the full profit on the short condor. Another key difference is that you receive a net credit rather than paying a net debit.

The short calls pose a risk of being exercised early, so you must pay particular attention to in-the-money calls with little time value remaining. The exercise of a call could upset the trade at a potentially critical moment, especially in the final few days of expiration, when pricing may be extra volatile.

Chapter 8

Troubleshooting Options Trading

Options magnify the market's moves, so every decision can be more costly if you're wrong or more profitable if you're right. You'll want to quickly learn how to make good decisions and avoid bad ones. As you trade, you're going to encounter any number of issues. Some are just the same old things faced by any trader—stocks that aren't performing like you expect or the market taking a dive just when you need it to stay flat or rise. You'll need to handle the setbacks that inevitably come with trading. That requires experience and a keen focus on learning and improving your trading process.

Beyond the market's moves, however, you're going to bring personal issues to trading, despite your best efforts. Emotions play a huge role in trading—not just the highs and lows that come with profits and losses but also the greed and fear that kick in when you see opportunity and risk. You need to prevent emotions from derailing your trading game, and that means you'll need to understand how emotions are driving your actions. Finally, it's important to set realistic goals so that you're not demanding results that you don't have the time or ability to deliver, or you can quickly damage your chances for success.

HOW TO PIVOT WHEN THE MARKET SHIFTS

Responding to Quick-Moving Trades

While the long-term direction of the stock market is higher, in the short term, stocks can move in any direction, and options traders need to plan for how to react when the unexpected happens. It's not just a question of stocks declining, though. If a stock moves up 10%, sending your call option up 200%, what do you do? You may never see that option price again, and you need to decide how to act. The nature of options means that you must tend to your trades actively, and you can close them literally every day the market is open.

The wasting nature of options means that time is a huge factor in your decision-making: Will the stock continue to move favorably by the option's expiration, or is it time to close out your option today? Stockholders have the luxury of waiting—for the next quarterly report, the next product, the turnaround—but time is constantly ticking down the value of options. You cannot idle when the market moves, and you need to be actively evaluating the risk in your positions against the potential reward. Not deciding to do something or deciding to do nothing have the same effect, but it's better to be actively watching your positions, even if you decide to hold on for another day.

Here's what to do when the market shifts and how to think about plotting a course of action.

BALANCE THE PROSPECTIVE
RISK AND REWARD

Your key task when the market shifts is to weigh the potential future gains against the current risks and then decide how to act. Everything that's happened in the past is done, and you can't change it. But you can always make decisions about the right future course while avoiding hanging on to the past and what might have been. The key question here is: At the current price, is this trade worth continuing to hold on to? To answer that question, you need to analyze the situation in some depth:

- **Is only your stock being affected, or is it the market as a whole?** If only your stock is affected, focus your analysis there. If the market is being affected—say, the economy is slowing or stocks may be running into a bear market—then it could make sense to close out multiple positions. In a bear or bull market, stocks may move regardless of their fundamentals, and every moment of delay may cost money across multiple positions.
- **How much time is left on the option?** An option with 18 months remaining offers a different proposition than one with only three weeks. It could make sense to ride out an option with a lot of life left, especially if it's a short-term fluctuation in that stock. For an option with a few weeks or months, it can make sense to take advantage of whatever pricing you can get now, especially if the option is out of the money.
- **Are your options out of the money or in the money, and how far?** An out-of-the-money option has a greater chance of expiring worthless than an in-the-money option, which still has intrinsic

value. An out-of-the-money option may quickly become a deep-out-of-the-money option, which may not even find a buyer or seller, so you may be stuck holding to expiration whether you like it or not.

- **How much higher or lower could the stock go before the option expires?** When the market is driven by greed or fear, stocks can go much higher or lower than you might reasonably expect.
- **Are you dealing with normal market fluctuations or is the stock ready to move?** Stocks often move a few percentage points in a week. So, is the move a normal fluctuation or something else? Near-the-money or out-of-the-money options may be worth closing if there's little time left. Options with intrinsic value may be worth holding if it's a normal gyration and the option has time to recover. If the stock is trending, it may be worth holding to see if you get more of that favorable move.

You'll need to consider these variables together to see whether it makes sense to continue holding an option or to close it. But the nature of options means that you must keep a close eye on risk so that you're being paid adequately. Trading options is tough. You will not "top-tick" or "bottom-tick" the options market, getting the highest sell price or the lowest buy price. Your profits will always be suboptimal relative to the most you could have made with the best decision.

Playing the Odds

You'll never know the best trading decision until time plays out. You're making educated guesses based on potential risk and reward. Yes, sometimes the stock does soar in the last week of a call option's existence, but most of the time it doesn't.

TRACKING POSITIONS AGAINST YOUR INVESTMENT THESIS

This book advocates using a fundamentals-led approach to trading options, so your investment thesis can help guide your decision-making too. If you determine a stock's move is related to the company, it's time to dig into your thesis and see whether it's playing out as expected:

- Is the company's business on track?
- Did the most recently reported quarter look great, but the stock dropped anyway?
- Could your investment thesis be wrong, and how?
- Where is the stock price relative to your estimate of its value?

For a company that's performing well and whose stock remains well below your estimate of its value, it may be worth holding on to call options despite a recent drop. It could even make sense to set up a new options position to take advantage of the stock's unfavorable move. But balance that against your position sizing and exposure. Depending on the conditions, it could make sense to take a loss and then set up a more favorable strategy on the same stock.

Whether up or down, every market move is a potential new opportunity. If the market dips, it's time to look for the next opportunity. But it's the same situation if the market rises and you close out your position. Sometimes the best opportunity is based on a stock you already own, and maybe even one you just lost on. As an options trader, you're spoiled for choice, compared to stock-only investors. Options offer way more choice than just the "buy-sell" of stocks, so there's always a profitable option trade out there. So, regardless of the market, always keep enough capital to trade another day.

HOW TO HANDLE SETBACKS

When Bad Trades Happen

Losses are part of the job as a trader, and there's not a trader alive who doesn't have a story about a painful loss. But the only way you can make a gain in trading is to put some money at risk, and as this book has emphasized repeatedly, options trading is a zero-sum game in which only one side can be a winner. While both sides of a trade think they're right, only one can be. Setbacks are just part of the bumpy terrain here, but it's vital that you learn to deal with them to become a better trader and so that these losses don't come to hurt your trading.

MINIMIZE YOUR LOSSES FIRST

Losses are painful, but the first place to begin is using strategies that minimize loss before it happens. This book has laid out many ways to reduce risk, including diversifying your options trades by time and strategy and keeping a tight rein on risks. But bad things happen to good traders, and the market can move unfavorably even when you're doing the right things. A setback is a time to go back to your trading process and figure out what isn't working and why. If you find the same types of things happening over and over, analyze what you're doing wrong and make a change to your trading plan. Stop the losses before they're losses.

REORIENT YOUR MINDSET
TO LEARNING

As a trader you need to get something from every trade, even if it's a losing trade. Each trade should help you build your expertise so that you develop a feel for an attractive risk-reward setup when you see it. Over time, you'll get a more intuitive sense for when to close out a trade and when to stick around. But to develop this mindset you'll need to analyze your trades and recognize accurately where you've made a mistake and how you can correct it in the future. It can be hard to look at your mistakes, but it's one of the best ways to get better. Learn from the mistake and try to avoid it in the future.

You're going to make losing trades, but a learning mindset can help you make fewer of them and refocus your attention from the setback to how to use a loss as a chance to improve.

TAKE YOUR LOSS AND MOVE ON

If you've evaluated a trade and it looks like you need to take a loss, then do so. It's typically better to close and take an 80% loss than ride the option to expiration and a 100% loss. It can be all too easy to get wrapped up in the trade because you don't want to take a loss, and you ride a loser to the bitter end. If you're coming to options after focusing mostly on stocks, the importance of taking a loss may not be as much emphasized, because holding on longer can often make sense for high-quality stocks, given their longer lifetimes. But options traders don't have that luxury. If you're down a lot and the risk-reward does not look favorable, a big loss is better than a total loss.

Close the position and then evaluate what you could have done differently over the course of the trade. Sometimes the answer is nothing. Other times, it may have made sense to close out when you got a favorable move earlier and you weren't paying attention or you made some error in judgment. Use that learning mindset and make your mistakes an opportunity to grow.

Process, Process, Process

As you're analyzing your closed trades, it's important to stay focused on your trading process. Bad trades can always happen with good process, so don't assume the process was bad just because you lost money. But, over time, developing a good process helps you reduce bad outcomes.

FOCUS ON RESILIENCE

In any human endeavor, the real difference between the long-term winners and losers is that the winners get back up, figure out what went wrong, and start striving again. It's the same in trading; you need to focus on both emotional and portfolio resilience. You've got to have the emotional fortitude to get back out there after a loss when you feel like doing anything but that. Sure, indulge yourself in a few days of feeling bad if you need to, but then you've got to have the resilience to adjust and get back to winning. Your key mantra here is: "What's the next right move?" Figure out your next right move to resume winning, whether that's adjusting your trading plan, finding new trading opportunities, or even taking a break, if that's what you need.

At the same time, make sure your portfolio is resilient too. What's the next right move there? You need to be able to take a loss and come back swinging, and you can't do that if you're taking too much risk or if you run out of capital. A resilient portfolio ensures that losses don't put you out of the game for good, even if you do suffer setbacks.

TAKE A BREAK FROM TRADING

If a loss or a series of losses rattles you too intensely, you may need a break from trading. If you're prone to emotionalize your trading, some time away from your screen may be the best thing for you. You don't necessarily have to stay away from options entirely—unless that's what you need—but don't place any trades. You can do research, review your trading process, find interesting opportunities, and perform other trading-related activities. These activities can keep your mind in the game and even reinvigorate you for when you do return. But give yourself time to settle down and figure out how you're going to move forward when you're trading. And don't rush back because you think you're missing out on great trades. The market will always offer great trades, but you need to be around with capital if you're going to profit on them.

Ultimately, a setback can be a rough experience, especially if you have a lot of money on the line. It's hard to not get emotional about it all, but it's vital that you don't let those emotions creep into your trading process. You'll end up making terrible trades and compounding your mistakes quickly. The next section delves into how to avoid letting emotions ruin your trading.

KEEPING EMOTIONS OUT OF TRADING

Don't Let Fear or Greed Get You

As good as a winning trade feels, losing money feels twice as bad, at least so the research on behavioral finance says. But whether you're winning or losing, it's vital to keep your emotions out of your trading process. Greed, fear, anger, elation—they can all affect your ability to rationally evaluate a trade opportunity and can have you setting up silly trades that offer poor returns.

Here are a few strategies for keeping emotions out of your trading and being more successful.

RECOGNIZE THAT EMOTIONS CAN AFFECT YOUR MINDSET

The people who are most likely to be fooled by their emotions are those who think they don't need to pay attention to them, including people who think they're great rational decision-makers. If you don't acknowledge that emotions can affect your trading decisions, you lay completely exposed to a trap. You won't see the emotional snare lying in wait, and worse—later, when you review what happened, you won't acknowledge that emotions played a role. You engage in what psychologists call cognitive dissonance, refusing to see the role played by emotions to avoid mental stress and instead blaming circumstances or bad luck.

Those who are best at rational decision-making recognize the role that emotions can play, even as they work to mitigate those effects. Pretending that you're not prone to emotional trading is setting you up for disaster because you won't try to prevent what's going to lead you to failure.

EMOTIONS ARE YOUR TELLTALE SIGNS TO REFOCUS

How do you know emotions are driving your trading? Easy—when you start feeling them. Pay attention if you feel giddy by all the money you're making or that "you can't lose." Similarly, if you feel angry or left out while everyone else seems to be making money, those could be signs. Feelings such as these indicate that you're getting emotionally wrapped up in your trading, and they're indicators that you need to refocus on your trading process. The goal is not to eliminate the emotion—everyone feels good with a win—but to mitigate them in your process. To do so, you'll need to watch how you respond emotionally and recognize when emotion is driving things.

WATCH OUT IF YOU'RE WINNING

Going to the championship as a first-year pro sports player is oftentimes worse for their career. That initial success makes what is a difficult feat seem easy and leads them into the false sense of what it takes to succeed, and so it is with options trading.

If you have a nice win on a few trades and feel the elation of that profit, options may seem easy to you. You're likely to go on to your next trades without doing enough work and avoiding the careful analysis of why and how your trade was successful. You could end up chasing those "easy wins" that end up being anything but easy without the right work and focus.

BEWARE REACTIVE DECISION-MAKING

When you lose money, it can be easy to want to jump back in and make another trade to win back that lost money, especially on the same stock. You've been dealt a blow, and you want to get in there and throw a punch right back. This can be a huge mistake. You may well be reacting to that loss and trying to make up for it with a subpar trade rather than finding a great risk-reward scenario for your next trade. Repeat this behavior, and you can quickly run up a string of losses. You need to step back, cool off, and then find the next right trade idea, wherever it is.

PLAN WHEN YOU'RE CALM

Planning your actions ahead of time can help you take emotion out of later decision-making in the "heat of battle." Determine your exit plan when you set up the trade, planning for both success and failure. Building a decision plan for both outcomes can make you balance the real possibilities of loss and gain rather than being starry-eyed about the potential profits.

Setting up your plan when you make a trade can keep you from getting hotheaded when you're staring down a 75% loss or exulting over a 300% gainer. It's all too easy to think that you'll hold longer for a bit more gain or for that loss to reverse a little bit. Find a trading plan and rules that work for you and don't talk yourself out of them when your emotions are running high.

AVOID SECOND-GUESSING YOURSELF

Regret for "the one that got away" can be crippling and lead you to try to correct the mistake next time out, even if the trade was profitable. Traders can have a nasty habit of looking at how a position performed and eating their heart out at a missed opportunity. Don't judge yourself on a lone outcome when you have a good, workable process that delivers results—it's unfair. You're right or wrong because your process is good or bad, not because the option moved some way. Sometimes too-risky decisions turn out okay, but often they don't. But you'll never know until events play out. If the risk-reward setup looked unfavorable at the time, understand that you made the decision on the data and the plan you had at the time. Don't fight the last war, because you'll end up losing.

When to Change It Up . . .

If you have a trading process in place, you're sticking to it because it's what keeps you making smart decisions under uncertainty. Still, if you're reviewing your decisions and discover that a different strategy would have consistently helped you, then maybe it's time to change things up.

STOP COMPARING YOUR RETURNS TO OTHERS'

When you're trading it can be all too easy to compare your results with what others are doing or how the market's performing, especially if everyone seems to be making money but you. This kind of comparison can set you up to be too aggressive or can make you feel envy or self-pity—all of which can harm your trading decisions. Tune out those potential sources of emotional energy, and then get refocused on your trading plan and make it even better.

SETTING REALISTIC GOALS

Right-Sizing Your Mindset for Success

You're on a roll; you keep making winning trades and steering clear of losing ones. It's been an amazing year, and if you keep going like this, you'll have millions of dollars stacked away in the next couple years. Even if your goals aren't quite so lofty yet, it can be all too easy to get into a mindset where you're demanding unrealistic outcomes from your trading. But any time you're dealing with market-based investments—stocks, funds, and especially options—you need to make sure your goals are realistic. Or you may pressure yourself into making risky trades that move you further from your goal. Realistic goals help you have a target to measure your progress and create a sustainable framework for success.

First, recognize when you're setting unrealistic goals, and then work toward actively setting realistic goals.

AVOID EXTRAPOLATING INTO THE FUTURE

You may have been on a run of luck, or the market may have been favoring your strategies, but it's important not to extrapolate successes into the future when making your goals. Your bankroll will not move up in a straight line, and you'll have wins and losses along the way that make your portfolio look lumpy. Even when you're mostly winning, your capital will grow in fits and starts.

WATCH OUT FOR GOALS THAT ARE MONEY-BASED

Trying to wring well-defined amounts of money from your trading is apt to lead to disaster. If your goal is to make $10,000 each month, you're going to start taking risks to make it happen and the risks may not be aligned with your temperament and trading process. When your only goal is a specific dollar amount and you're dead set on it, you'll abandon your trading strategies and process that have been working for you. A "soft target" focused on your process, such as maintaining a 75% win rate on each month's trades, can be more useful than a "must hit" dollar goal, such as making $1,000 each month.

BEWARE OUTCOME-BASED GOALS

If you focus on a specific outcome (such as money), it can be easy to lose sight of how valuable your trading process is to your success. When you focus on the process and not a specific outcome, you'll put the emphasis on improving what truly drives your success.

HOW TO SET REALISTIC GOALS

None of this is to say that you shouldn't have goals—money-based or otherwise—but that the goals need to be aligned with your trading process and temperament. Here are some key things to consider:

What do you want from options trading? A little extra income, lottery-like returns, or something in between? Consider what you want from trading in the short term and long term. Learning how everything works and making a few trades each month can be good short-term goals. You can focus on mastering specific options strategies and working them into your trading process. As your skills develop, you'll probably want to expand your goals. However you proceed, your goals are personal and specific to you and what you want from your trading.

Do your goals match your temperament? Options trading has plenty of risk, and it's not for everyone. But some strategies are better suited to a trader's risk tolerance. If you want to generate income and not take big risks, options let you do that. If you want to hit the lottery, you can take the big risks too. Or some combination of the two. If your goal is to generate relatively safe income, and you're buying options instead of selling them, you're taking the wrong tack. The only wrong answer here is if you're setting up a strategy that you're not comfortable with and that doesn't align with your goals. While taking big risks may seem glamorous, the world's best investors are risk averse. They're willing to take risks but only if they're being well paid for them.

How much time do you have for trading? Goals such as making a certain amount of money or progressing quickly require a lot of time. You'll need to do the research to make smart trades, you'll need to monitor them closely as they reach milestones such as expiration, and even placing trades can take a surprising amount of time when you're running a portfolio of money. If you don't have much time to devote to options, that's fine. But be sure that your goals align with the time you're willing and able to devote to trading. In options, it can be useful to go slowly, so you shouldn't feel compelled to spend huge amounts of time, but your progress will be slower.

How much money are you working with? You can't expect to make thousands a month if you're working with a $500 bankroll. If your goal is money-based, it must fit with the capital in your account.

If you're starting small, you may be tempted to make riskier trades to meet a loftier profit goal. But work within your limits. As you build your cash stack, you can increase your goal.

How will you work on your trading process? One of the most important ways to set realistic goals is to improve your trading process so that you know what's realistic. Your process includes everything you do from A to Z—how you find ideas, analyze them, set up the trade, close it, review your trades, and so on. You'll need time to do all of this, and the more experience you have to work with, the more you'll be able to develop your expertise and refine your process. It can be useful to analyze both successes and failures so that you see what's working and what isn't, and how you can change your process to get better results. Working on your process is how you align your ability to what is a realistic goal.

How will you stick to your trading process with a money-based goal? The danger with a specific financial goal is that you'll abandon a workable trading process to hit the goal. If you usually sell options, maybe you'll try to buy them to meet the goal and take on more risk. As soon as a financial goal becomes something that encourages you to stray from your trading process, you need to swiftly refocus on your process and then adjust the goal. A goal exists to help you improve your process, so you can't abandon the process to meet the goal.

Options Speed Limit: Your Speed

In options trading, you can move at any speed. You decide the risks you're willing to run and how much you're willing to pay or be paid for them. If you don't like a trade, you don't have to do it. Keep your goals aligned with what you need.

INDEX

Account (brokerage), setting up, 38

Advantages of options, 17–19

American-style options, 77–78

Assets, underlying, defined, 40

Bear call spreads, 205, 219–23

Bear put spreads, 205, 214–18

Black-Scholes pricing model, 59–61, 74

Break from trading, taking, 272

Brokerage account, setting up, 38

Buffett, Warren, 22, 29

Bull call spreads, 205, 209–13

Bull put spreads, 205, 224–28

Butterfly spreads
long butterfly spread with calls, 240–44
long iron butterfly spread, 249–53
short butterfly spread with calls, 245–48

Call options
defined/explained, 13–14, 42

how they work, 44–46

profit on, 46–47

put-call parity, 72–77

put options and, 13–14 (*See also* Put options)

rewards and risks, 44–48

Calls, strategies with
bear call spreads, 205, 219–23
bull call spreads, 205, 209–13
covered calls, 36, 85–86, 154–58, 235
long butterfly spread with calls, 240–44
long calendar spread with calls, 206, 229–33
long condor spread with calls, 254–58
long diagonal spread with calls, 207, 234–38
short butterfly spread with calls, 245–48
short calendar spread with calls, 206
short condor spread with calls, 259–63
short diagonal spread with calls, 207

Chain, options, 97–100

Closing positions. *See* Trades, closing out

Collar, 194–98

Commissions, 12, 36–37, 202, 239

Condor spreads
long condor spread with calls, 254–58
short condor spread with calls, 259–63

Contracts
cost (premium) of, 41
defined, 41
exercising, 41–42
need for, 10
option types, 13–14 (*See also* Call options; Put options)
placing trades and, 103
risks/rewards (*See* Risks and rewards)

Covered calls, 36, 85–86, 154–58, 235

Cycle, options, 100–101

Decision-making, emotions and, 275. *See also* Emotions

Deep in the money, 54, 57, 59, 63, 68–69, 77

Delta, 63, 65, 118

Derivatives, options as, 9

Diagonal spreads, 204, 206–7

Disadvantages of options, 19–21

Dividends, 73–74, 77

Emotions
    decision making and, 275
    keeping out of trading, 273–77
    mindset and, 273–74
    refocusing indicator, 274
    winning and, 274–75
European-style options, 77–78, 80–81
Exercising options, 14–15
Exiting trades. *See* Trades, closing out
Expiration of options, 41, 78–79
Extrinsic value. *See* Time value

Failure, avoiding, 119–23

Gamma, 63, 65
Goals, setting, 278–81
Greeks, 42, 62–66

Hedging, 18, 65, 118, 157, 201, 234, 235
Horizontal spreads, 204, 205–6

Insurance, options as, 19, 21, 24–25, 41, 143, 162, 220. *See also* Protective puts
In-the-money (ITM) options
    deep in the money, 54, 57, 59, 63, 68–69, 77

defined/explained, 45–46, 54–55
    example, 50–51
    volatility and, 69–70
Intrinsic value, 55–56, 57, 69, 266–67
Investing. *See also* Strategies *entries*; Trades, closing out; Trades, placing; Trading options
    basics of, 30–34
    building options portfolio, 114–18
    failures to avoid, 119–23
    importance of understanding, 34
    stock valuation and, 31–34 (*See also* Intrinsic value; Time value; Value of options)

Legging into trades, 106–9. *See also* Multi-leg trades
Leverage of options, 15–16
Long strategies
    long butterfly spread with calls, 240–44
    long calendar spread with calls, 206, 229–33
    long calendar spread with puts, 206
    long calls, 125–30
    long condor spread with calls, 254–58
    long diagonal spread with calls, 207, 234–38
    long diagonal spread with puts, 207

long iron butterfly spread, 249–53
    long puts, 137–42
    long straddle, 174–78
    long strangle, 184–88
    synthetic long, 164–68
Losses
    focusing on resilience and, 271–72
    handling setbacks, 269–72
    magnitude potential, 20–21, 23
    minimizing, 269
    reorienting mindset to learning, 270
    risks/rewards and (*See* Risks and rewards)
    sensitivity to asset prices and, 23
    taking and moving on, 270–71

Multi-leg trades, 84–86, 102, 105, 106–7, 113, 150–51, 183, 239–44

Options
    about: fundamentals overview, 39; overview of, 8; this book and, 6–7
    advantages and disadvantages, 17–21
    expectations of buy/selling, 14
    expiring worthless, 15
    flexibility of, 106
    how they work, 13–16
    leverage of, 15–16
    risks/rewards of (*See* Risks and rewards)

settlement of, 14–15
strategies for (*See*
    Strategies *entries*)
styles of, 77–81
terms to know, 40–42
Out-of-the-money (OTM)
    options
    balancing risk/reward
        and, 266–67
    deep out of the money,
        68–69
    defined/explained, 45,
        54–55
    time value, closing
        trades and, 112

Pivoting when market
    shifts, 265–68
Planning. *See also*
    Strategies *entries*
    avoiding second-
        guessing, 276
    emotions and, 273–77
    setting realistic goals,
        278–81
    when calm, 275
Premium, defined, 41
Pricing. *See* Value of
    options
Protective puts, 159–63,
    197
Put options
    call options and, 13–14
        (*See also* Call options)
    defined/explained,
        13–14, 42–43, 49
    how they work, 49–51
    profit on, 51–52
    put-call parity, 72–77
    rewards and risks, 52–53
    strategy example,
        95–96

Puts, strategies with
    bear put spreads, 205,
        214–18
    bull put spreads, 205,
        224–28
    long calendar spread
        with puts, 206
    long diagonal spread
        with puts, 207
    long puts, 137–42
    protective puts, 159–63,
        197
    short calendar spread
        with puts, 206
    short diagonal spread
        with puts, 207
    short puts, 143–48

Refocusing, emotions
    and, 274
Resilience, focusing on,
    271–72
Returns, improving. *See*
    Strategies *entries*;
    Troubleshooting trading
Rho, 64
Risks and rewards
    about: overview of,
        10–11, 22–23
    balancing amid
        shifting market,
        265–68
    call options, 44–48
    hedging, 18
    limiting risk, 19, 24–25
    loss potential, 20–21, 23
    trading risk, 18

Seller results, 16
Setbacks, handling, 269–
    72. *See also* Losses

Settlement of options,
    14–15
Shifting market, pivoting
    in, 265–68
Short strategies
    short butterfly spread
        with calls, 245–48
    short calendar spread
        with calls, 206
    short calendar spread
        with puts, 206
    short calls, 131–36
    short condor spread
        with calls, 259–63
    short diagonal spread
        with calls, 207
    short diagonal spread
        with puts, 207
    short puts, 143–48
    short straddle, 179–83
    short strangle, 189–93
    synthetic short, 169–73
Side bets, 12, 41
Single-leg options, 82–84
Spreads. *See* Strategies,
    spread options
Stocks
    buying "insurance"
        on (*See* Insurance,
        options as; Protective
        puts)
    getting better prices
        on, 25
    key terms to know,
        40–42
    valuation factors and
        prices, 31–34
Straddles
    long straddle, 174–78
    short straddle, 179–83
Strangles
    long strangle, 184–88

short strangle, 189–93
Strategies. *See also*
    Trading options;
    specific strategy types
    immediately following
        analyzing company,
            88–91
        determine stock
            direction, 91–92
        finding/selecting right
            strategy, 93–96
        investment thesis/
            analysis, 88–92
        options cycle
            mechanics and,
            100–101
        practical example,
            95–96
        reading options chain,
            97–100
Strategies, basic
    about: core four
        options, 149–51;
        ego and, 151–52; not
        overlooking, 149–52;
        overview of, 124–52
    backbone of options
        trading, 149–52
    long calls, 125–30
    long puts, 137–42
    short calls, 131–36
    short puts, 143–48
Strategies, intermediate
    and advanced, 153–98.
    See also Strategies,
    spread options;
    Strategies, spread
    options (multi-leg)
        about: overview of, 153
        collar, 194–98
        covered calls, 36,
            85–86, 154–58, 235

long straddle, 174–78
long strangle, 184–88
protective puts, 159–63,
    197
short straddle, 179–83
short strangle, 189–93
synthetic long, 164–68
synthetic short, 169–73
troubleshooting (*See*
    Troubleshooting
    trading)
Strategies, spread options
    about: overview of,
        199; pros and cons of,
        200–203, 208
    advantages and
        disadvantages,
        200–203
    bear call spreads, 205,
        219–23
    bear put spreads, 205,
        214–18
    bull call spreads, 205,
        209–13
    bull put spreads, 205,
        224–28
    diagonal spreads, 204,
        206–7
    horizontal spreads,
        204, 205–6
    long calendar spread
        with calls, 206, 229–33
    long calendar spread
        with puts, 206
    long diagonal spread
        with calls, 207, 234–38
    long diagonal spread
        with puts, 207
    other hybrid options
        strategies using
        spreads, 207–8
    short calendar spread

with calls, 206
short calendar spread
    with puts, 206
short diagonal spread
    with calls, 207
short diagonal spread
    with puts, 207
troubleshooting (*See*
    Troubleshooting
    trading)
vertical spreads, 204–6
Strategies, spread options
(multi-leg), 239–63
    about: overview of, 239
    long butterfly spread
        with calls, 240–44
    long condor spread
        with calls, 254–58
    long iron butterfly
        spread, 249–53
    short butterfly spread
        with calls, 245–48
    short condor spread
        with calls, 259–63
    troubleshooting (*See*
        Troubleshooting
        trading)
Strike price, defined, 40–41
Styles of options, 77–81
Success. *See* Goals,
    setting; Planning;
    Strategies *entries*
Surprises, lack of, 25
Synthetic long, 164–68
Synthetic short, 169–73

Taxes, 82–86
Theta, 63, 64–66, 68–69, 71
Time limits, 10
Time value
    closing trades and,
        111–12

defined/explained, 47, 56

horizontal spreads and, 205–6

nonlinear movement and, 67

pricing dynamic, moneyness and, 56–57

time decay, volatility and, 68–69

Trades, closing out
about: mechanical selling, 113; netting out trades, 113

how and when to exit, 14–15, 110–13

risk-reward evaluation and, 112

Trades, placing, 102–5
flexibility of options and, 106

legging into trades, 106–9 (*See also* Multi-leg trades)

order-entry pitfalls to avoid, 104–5

Trading options. *See also* Strategies *entries*
about: ego and, 151–52; overview of, 87

active management requirement, 12

brokerage account for, 38

considerations, deciding if right for you, 26–29

as derivatives, 9

handling setbacks, 269–72

pivoting when market shifts, 265–68

profit paths, 11

qualifying for options approval, 35–38

risks/rewards (*See* Risks and rewards)

setting realistic goals, 278–81

side bets, 12, 41

speed of, 281

taking break from, 272

time limits and, 10

troubleshooting (*See* Troubleshooting trading)

what you need for, 35–38

winners, losers and, 11–12

Troubleshooting trading, 264–81
about: overview of, 264

handling setbacks, 269–72

keeping emotions out, 273–77

pivoting when market shifts, 265–68

Uncovered calls, 131, 220–21, 223

Value of options
about: "moneyness" and, 54

Black-Scholes pricing model, 59–61, 74

components of price, 58–59

dividends and, 73–74, 77

far- and near-term options and, 71

the Greeks and, 42, 62–66

how prices move, 67–71

implied volatility and, 69–70

in-the-money (ITM) options, 54

intrinsic value vs time value, 54–57 (*See also* Intrinsic value; Time value)

key drivers to prices, 62–66

nonlinear movement and, 67

pricing dynamics, moneyness and, 56–57

what options are worth, 58–61

Vega, 63–64, 65

Vertical spreads, 204–6

Wash-sale rule, 86

Worthless, options expiring as, 15

Zero-day options, 79–80

ABOUT THE AUTHOR

James Royal, PhD, cut his teeth on stock investing during the dot-com bubble and has traded options for nearly as long. He is the author of *The Zen of Thrift Conversions*, which details the investment opportunity in hidden bank stocks, and he serves as the principal writer on investing at Bankrate, where his work has been cited across major media. Dr. Royal believes in the power of financial education to help individuals make smart decisions that significantly improve their lives.